"Michelle C. Hughes masterfully power of core dispositions, centering their place at the heart of educational practice. Drawing on research and rich personal experiences, Hughes provides an inspiring guide for educators, illuminating the path with essential dispositions that not only reignite passion but also empower both teachers and students. This book is refreshing and validating, positive and inspiring, intellectual and reflective – a new classic that I'll revisit time and time again."

Susan Salcido, *Santa Barbara County Schools,*
Santa Barbara, California, USA

"Brimming with hope-filled stories and practical strategies, this book elucidates 13 essential educator dispositions and invites readers to allow professional dispositions to permeate their hearts, penetrate their minds, pervade their practice, and promote holistic flourishing."

Carrie R. Wall, *Pepperdine University, Malibu, California, USA*

"As someone working in faculty development, I see firsthand how curious, resilient, and hopeful teachers can directly shape the outcomes that help students to thrive. Hughes draws on her weighty experience as a secondary teacher, administrator, researcher, and college faculty to show that dispositions can be taught. Not only is the author the most motivating of cheerleaders—offering high-fives throughout—she reminds us why such practices bring light to the vocation of teaching. This book is for those who have felt discouraged or overwhelmed as teachers; you will find light here."

Rachel Rains Winslow, *George Fox University,*
Newberg, Oregon, USA

"In a time when teaching seems to become more challenging by the day, Michelle C. Hughes has given educators a gift. Her book is thoroughly grounded in research and she writes in an invitational and personal tone that will leave her readers feeling like they can grow into and teach out of the dispositions she explores. Without a gram of hesitation, I recommend this book to all educators."

Ken Badley, *Tyndale University, Toronto, Ontario, Canada*

Dispositions Are a Teacher's Greatest Strength

Dispositions Are a Teacher's Greatest Strength will fuel and reignite your classroom practice. Focusing on 13 dispositions specific to teaching, this book encourages educators to identify, reflect, and develop their dispositions, attitudes, and self-awareness to flourish in the profession. Emphasizing pedagogical knowledge and skills, this text serves as an affirmation of a teacher's commitment to challenging, complex, and rewarding work. It invites educators to consider what a unique privilege it is to teach—to dive into reading and reflection, creating space, and embracing dispositions as a teacher's greatest strength. Each chapter focuses on one of 13 teaching dispositions—such as curiosity, adaptability, gratitude, resilience, and courage—and offers:

◆ definitions and contexts for the disposition of focus;
◆ concrete applications for teachers to practice and develop dispositions with reader-friendly examples and practical strategies;
◆ a "pause and reflect" section with questions and space for professional reflection.

This book serves as a love letter to educators everywhere: teachers in K-12, administrators in K-12, higher education faculty, pre-service programs and students. *Dispositions Are a Teacher's Greatest Strength* reminds teachers of the significant work they do by putting dispositions at the forefront of their daily work.

Michelle C. Hughes is an enthusiastic and passionate educator. Throughout her 34-year career, she taught junior high school English, worked as a high school administrator, and served as a faculty member in Westmont College's Education Department in Santa Barbara, CA, USA.

Also Available from Routledge
Eye on Education
(www.routledge.com/k-12)

Joyful Resilience as Educational Practice: Transforming
Teaching Challenges into Opportunities
Michelle C. Hughes and Ken Badley

Your First Year: How to Survive and Thrive as a
New Teacher, 2nd edition
Todd Whitaker, Madeline Whitaker Good, and
Katherine Whitaker

The Heart-Centered Teacher: Restoring Hope, Joy, and
Possibility in Uncertain Times
Regie Routman

Dear School Leader: 50 Motivational Quotes and Anecdotes
that Affirm Your Purpose and Your Impact
Brad Johnson

Pause, Ponder, and Persist in the Classroom: How Teachers
Turn Challenges into Opportunities for Impact
Julie Schmidt Hasson

Dispositions Are a Teacher's Greatest Strength

Mindful Pedagogical Practices to Develop Self-Awareness to Flourish in the Classroom

Michelle C. Hughes

Routledge
Taylor & Francis Group

NEW YORK AND LONDON

Designed cover image: wabeno / Getty Images

First published 2024
by Routledge
605 Third Avenue, New York, NY 10158

and by Routledge
4 Park Square, Milton Park, Abingdon, Oxon, OX14 4RN

Routledge is an imprint of the Taylor & Francis Group, an informa business

ISBN: 978-1-032-45979-0 (hbk)
ISBN: 978-1-032-45759-8 (pbk)
ISBN: 978-1-003-37953-9 (ebk)

DOI: 10.4324/9781003379539

Typeset in Palatino
by KnowledgeWorks Global Ltd.

I dedicate this book to the students and teachers that I have known and learned from through the years. It has been an honor to work with each of you; you are the inspiration for this book. You have modeled and shared the dispositions I hold dear and my heart smiles when I think of you.

Contents

About the Author

Michelle C. Hughes, Ed.D., is an enthusiastic educator and author who is passionate about teaching and learning alongside her students. Throughout her 34-year career, she taught junior high school English, worked as a high school administrator, and served as a faculty member in Westmont College's Education Department in Santa Barbara, CA. While at Westmont College, she taught and supervised student teachers and served several terms as the department chair.  She was honored with the college's Bruce and Adaline Bare Teacher of the Year Award for the Social Sciences in 2013. Her research and writing thoughtfully examines teaching dispositions or the postures, attitudes, and heart skills needed for professional flourishing. Michelle is also the co-editor of *Joyful Resilience as Educational Practice: Turning Challenges into Opportunities* (Routledge, 2022).

Preface

Teachers First

I have appointed myself the president of the Teaching Dispositions Fan Club. In reality, there isn't such a club, but if there was, I would be its president. Dispositions have always played an integral role in my professional life and they have been the focus of my scholarship for the last 15 years. Among the multitude of hats that teachers like you and I wear, our dispositions (and the heart work around them) are foundational to the wide-ranging work we do as educators. Teaching *is* heart, mind, and soul work. Dispositions—the harder-to-measure postures, attitudes, and commitments of the heart—are essential fuel for teachers to flourish in the classroom.

Cultivating core dispositions such as inclusion, reflection, empathy, and courage is a priority in most pre-service programs in the United States; however, as beginning teachers adapt to the challenges of their first classrooms, dispositions can be easily forgotten. Sadly, the urgent demands of classroom life can drain a teacher's energy and spirit, leaving little time and space for cultivating dispositions. Dispositions often take a back seat to the lesson plans, classroom management, conferences, and countless other demands placed on a teacher's time and energy. Teacher dispositions, as defined by the Council for the Accreditation of Educator Preparation, are "the habits of professional action and moral commitments that underlie an educator's performance" (2016, p. 6). It is my hope that reading *Dispositions Are a Teacher's Greatest Strength: Mindful Pedagogical Practices to Develop Self-Awareness to Flourish in the Classroom*, will give teachers from K-12 to higher education encouragement and reignited enthusiasm for the meaningful work that they do. The following chapters explore 13 powerful dispositions through story, strategy, and self-reflection.

During my 34 years in education, I served as a junior high teacher, high school administrator, and pre-service program professor. My professional experiences sparked curiosity and research around dispositional strength and as a result, I offer *Dispositions Are a Teacher's Greatest Strength* to teachers everywhere. Each chapter provides the context for each of the 13 dispositions. Each chapter also offers concrete application for teachers to practice and develop dispositions through examples and practical strategies. Lastly, each chapter invites educators to "pause and reflect" with questions and space for intentional reflection.

Dispositions Are a Teacher's Greatest Strength moves readers from learning about each disposition to considering and reflecting on how they can identify, develop, and increase self-awareness in relation to the disposition. Each chapter prompts readers to identify how teachers, as individuals and colleagues, foster and practice each of these 13 dispositions. Ultimately, I've found through research and experience that when teachers identify, seek, and foster dispositions in practice, they will transfer dispositions to their students (Hughes, 2014, 2020). Investing in practices that enable teachers to develop dispositions to meet the needs of their students is a winning combination (Wenzel & Roberts, 2014). As with so many facets of teaching, there is a profound overflow effect when teachers identify, seek, and foster dispositions in practice; students then see the dispositions modeled and they will often adopt dispositional habits for themselves.

Once a young teacher lands a first teaching position, they are more or less required to learn all the aspects of the job "on the fly." The support system found in a pre-service program with hands-on professors, student teaching supervisors, and cooperating teachers all but disappears when a young teacher starts their first job. Subsequently, much of a teacher's growth and goal setting becomes self-directed. As teachers develop, there is an increasing need to build an educator's self-awareness and promote reflection as part of professional development; by doing so, educators are encouraged to acknowledge their emotions, responses, and job performance (Kennedy, 2023). Self-awareness benefits individuals making choices, setting goals, *and* dispositional awareness strengthens teachers' decision-making. Because teachers make countless decisions each day, focusing on developing dispositional awareness becomes a worthy professional priority.

In recent years, challenges in education intensified due to the COVID-19 pandemic; concerns around mental health, learning gaps, equity, and student achievement were thrust into the spotlight. Because of the unusual circumstances, teachers became more in tune with their own personal and professional needs. I must stress that with record rates of burnout, paying attention to teachers' mental health needs is as necessary as paying attention to students' mental health needs. Unfortunately, there is often a disconnect when schools and districts focus solely on student needs without addressing teacher needs (Liabenow & Philibert, 2022). If teacher needs are not addressed, students are ultimately impacted; therefore, helping teachers thrive becomes critical so that they can stay focused on students, their greatest priority.

In response to the current pressures and stressors educators experience, this book frames a teacher's daily work with dispositions at the forefront, expanding professional toolboxes and reaffirming the significance of a teacher's work. Focusing on the challenges of teacher stress and wellness can be attended to with intention. Well-being practices such as breathing, seeing a counselor, accessing training and professional development, and even simple provisions like meals and snacks can make a difference for teachers. Moreover, mitigating burnout and sustaining teachers' careers with wellness support can help teachers flourish in an increasingly challenging profession. We know that a teacher's job isn't to fix students but to provide opportunities for them to become their best selves (Mullikin, 2023). If we focus on teacher well-being, I predict students will feel the ripple effects.

Taking Action

Social and emotional learning or SEL has been a focus in education for many years, but post-pandemic, SEL has taken center stage in many schools. Social and emotional learning refers to the process of developing self-awareness, interpersonal skills, and self-control for school and life. Students, families, teachers, and school communities are all part of a larger system that shapes and develops students. SEL highlights a variety of competencies to support students' psychological health. In addition, social-emotional competence translates into results regarding student engagement, problem-solving skills, higher grade point averages, self-awareness, and self-regulation. In particular, educators with strong social emotional competence foster positive relationships with students (Bergin et al., 2023). They not only manage their own emotions but seek to understand others' emotions. Developing emotional intelligence typically results in increased self-awareness (Thompson et al., 2023) because when teachers are cared for, students are cared for, which impacts students' students' well-being, students' achievement, and teachers' well-being. These outcomes reinforce the need to develop teacher dispositions—for example, cultivating dispositions like empathy, found in Chapter 4, promote positive relationships that will serve teachers and students in and beyond the K-12 classroom. During the pandemic, teachers were forced to assess, reassess, and function with increased loving care for others; caring and how to care during a unique time in history became the focus (Stice, 2021, p. 2). Educators responded, found strengths and abilities in themselves that they were unaware of, and attended to others with immense care.

The field of education traditionally prioritizes outcomes for students over those for teachers; however, one set of researchers suggests fostering a climate conducive for differentiated teacher learning with a specific framework for professional development (Mausbach & Kazmierczak, 2023). The framework acknowledges that teachers don't all come from the same place or have the same experiences. Consequently, it is critical for schools to have shared learning goals that can be differentiated for particular teachers or groups of teachers. Just as we value students' strengths and differences, valuing teachers' strengths and differences can help teachers feel seen and heard. Nurturing professional teaching dispositions is a key component for honoring a teacher's individuality and gifts. Developing dispositions can strengthen teacher skills and attitudes that affirm a teacher's purpose and help them grow and thrive. Honoring teachers, their experiences, and knowledge with professional opportunities for growth can also enhance a school's climate and experiences for students. As I spend time in local classrooms in my community, I notice that teachers are craving affirmation more than ever: affirmation for their commitment to the profession, for the expertise they possess and share, and for their care for students. I firmly believe that harnessing the power of dispositions in practice can empower teachers in the short-term, and more importantly, foster habits for teachers to thrive professionally in the long-term.

Reading *Dispositions Are a Teacher's Greatest Strength* can serve as a form of self-care or a gift to one's teacher self. In the same way that spiritual practices like meditation and prayer can lessen an individual's stress, cultivating dispositions and dispositional habits can have a similar effect. Dispositions can inform teacher mindsets and actions whether a teacher is new to the profession or is a veteran teacher (Talley, 2020). I find that when I intentionally focus on specific dispositions, they become more than just a list of behaviors; instead, they become a means, a pathway, or a channel that energizes me and stimulates my heart and mind, often producing a sense of internal restoration within myself and my work. The process itself brings me renewal. I invite all educators to read, reflect, and consider what a unique privilege it is to teach.

Whether you choose to read this book alone or in a book club with others, I encourage you to dive into each chapter with a mindset that embraces dispositions, the heart skills, explored in this book. *Dispositions Are a Teacher's Greatest Strength* serves not as a how-to book, but as a validation of a teacher's commitment to a rewarding, challenging, and complex profession. The book does not ask readers to sympathize with teachers, but instead invites readers to ponder, reflect, and engage constructively with a collection of dispositions that honor the profession and all it requires. My intent for each chapter is to reassure and encourage educators and administrators in K-12, higher education, and pre-service programs. The personal anecdotes and stories shared throughout the book are my own experiences. I humbly recognize that I am not wiser than my colleagues or readers; I write from my own professional perspective knowing that my readers may have more expertise and knowledge than I have. I sincerely hope you will embrace the 13 dispositions in *Dispositions Are a Teacher's Greatest Strength* and will relish reflecting on your own professional journey.

Dive into Dispositions for Strength

Many educators view society's level of expectation for teachers as impossible to meet. Teachers are not saints; yet, they are often expected to love the job and at the same time deal with countless challenges such as trauma, poverty, and student behavior. These are the professional realities that are often viewed as simply part of the job. Educator Elizabeth Dampf acknowledges that there is a cultural illusion that teachers have to do it all and be it all. Teachers are expected to be self-sacrificing counselors and psychologists, food providers, and curriculum experts who don't complain but keep trying because they love students. Hence, it's not a surprise that there can be a disconnect between the passion and skills required; being a loving teaching or being passionate about teaching is not the same as being an effective teacher. According to Dampf, changing the conversation to how intelligent, skilled, and knowledgeable teachers are emerges as essential for educators to take charge of and own their attitudes for the profession (2022). Dispositions can be a vehicle to do this, to strengthen practice and affirm the heart skills that teachers embrace and model every day.

In my pre-service program at the college, my faculty team strives to prepare teachers for meaningful *and* lengthy careers. Integrating and intentionally paying attention to professional dispositions reaps benefits. And, highlighting and demonstrating dispositions can energize and sustain teachers for a lengthy career (Hughes, 2020). Through several studies, my research affirms that educators need to create space for dispositions, or the intangible attitudes of the heart, because dispositions can help us grow and mature as educators (Hughes, 2014, 2020). Recent research suggests that nurturing habits of mind "creates capacity to recognize and apply dispositional thinking to curriculum and the unpredictable challenges and opportunities educators a school faces" (Costa et al., 2021, p. 58). The more teachers and students "focus on and grapple with the habits of mind, the more these dispositions become internalized in their hearts, minds and behaviors" (p. 62). And as educators recognize and nurture dispositions, they build greater self-awareness and can put them into practice in the classroom (Costa & Kallick, 2014).

For me, the practice of researching, discussing, learning about, and writing about dispositions connects me on a deeper level to my students, to the profession, to my colleagues. When I intentionally make a choice to take time to consider dispositions that I hold dear, my heart and soul fill up. This practice is restorative because I am reminded of who I am as a scholar, an educator, a practitioner, and a colleague. Making a conscious choice to pursue a particular disposition strengthens and sustains me. Courage, for example, is a disposition that comes to mind as I think about the work of a teacher. Seeking, naming, and recognizing courage in my work grounds me as a professional and give me hope. It is not a surprise that teachers need a healthy dose of courage to embrace the emotionally challenging and rigorous work; making the decision to teach necessitates courage (Palmer, 2017). Chapter 11 addresses the disposition of courage in more detail.

As you read ahead, I urge you to take time to invest (and in some cases reinvest) in yourselves. Teaching is full of paradoxes; one day a teacher may feel elated about student engagement from a class discussion and the next day the same teacher may feel deflated due to a student's misbehavior. As educators, we have so much to offer others; yet, we need to intentionally create space for our own restoration (Brown, 2022). As a community of educators, lifelong learners, and scholars, let's seek opportunities to grow. Let's be courageous and intentional with our professional lives and our scholarship. Let's concentrate on the heart of teaching and the relationships between teachers, students, and school leaders that will grow us professionally (Hope, 2022). This book is designed to do just that; this book is written for you.

We often hear that knowledge is power; I believe dispositions are power too; dispositions open our hearts and elevate our professionalism. I wholeheartedly invite you to journey with me and join my Teaching Dispositions Fan Club.

References

Bergin, C., Cipriano, C., Wanless, S. B., & Barnes, T. B. (2023). Five key questions educators ask about SEL. *Kappan.* https://kappanonline.org/sel-questions-bergin-cipriano-wanless-barnes/

Brown, B. (2022). *Rising strong: How the ability to reset transforms the way we live, love, parent, and lead.* Random House.

Costa, A. L., & Kallick, B. (2014). *Dispositions: Reframing teaching and learning.* Corwin.

Costa, A. L., Kallick, B., & Zmuda, A. G. (2021). Building a culture of efficacy with habits of mind. *Educational Leadership, 79*(3), 57–62. https://www.ascd.org/el/articles/building-a-culture-of-efficacy-with-habits-of-mind

Council for the Accreditation of Educator Preparation (2016). In TASC Model Core Teaching Standards (p. 6). https://caepnet.org/glossary?letter=D

Dampf, E. (2022). It's about skillsets and support, not sainthood. *Educational Leadership, 80*(2). https://www.ascd.org/el/articles/its-about-skillsets-and-support-not-sainthood

Hope, M. (2022). Prioritizing connection. *Educational Leadership, 80*(2), 50–55. https://www.ascd.org/el/articles/prioritizing-connection

Hughes, M. C. (2014). *One pre-service program's dispositional efforts revealed.* [Doctoral dissertation, George Fox University]. http://digitalcommons.georgefox.edu/edd/31

Hughes, M. C. (2020). Dispositions: Real-time active practice. In P. Shotsberger, & C. Freytag (Eds.), *How shall we then care? A Christian educator's guide to caring for self, learners, colleagues, and community* (pp. 137–158). Wipf and Stock.

Kennedy, K. (2023). Growing from the seeds of leadership. *Principal, 102*(4), 36–39. https://www.naesp.org/resource/growing-from-the-seeds-of-leadership/

Liabenow, P., & Philibert, C. T. (2022). Two tracks toward wellness. *Principal, 102*(1), 22–25. https://www.naesp.org/resource/two-tracks-toward-wellness/

Mausbach, A., & Kazmierczak, K. M. (2023). Meeting teachers where they are. https://kappanonline.org/meeting-teachers-mausbach-kazmierczak/

Mullikin, J. (2023). Simplify the data points examined to pursue continuous improvement. *Principal, 102*(4), 17–19. https://naesp.ygsclicbook.com/pubs/principal/2023/marchapril-2023/live/index.html#p=18

Palmer, P. J. (2017). *The courage to teach. Exploring the inner landscape of a teacher's life.* Jossey-Bass.

Stice, E. (2021). Loving education in the time of COVID. *Front Porch Republic.* https://www.frontporchrepublic.com/2021/10/loving-education-in-the-time-of-covid

Talley, S. (2020). In P. Shotsberger & C. Freytag (Eds.), *How shall we then care? A Christian educator's guide to caring for self, learners, colleagues, and community* (pp. 159–173). Wipf and Stock.

Thompson, A., Travers, A., & Gomez, J. (2023). Lean in on four leadership traits, part 2. *Principal, 102*(4), 44–45. https://www.naesp.org/resource/lean-in-on-four-leadership-traits-part-2/

Wenzel, A., & Roberts, J. (2014). Coaching teacher dispositions. *Association for Middle Level Education.* https://www.amle.org/coaching-teacher-dispositions

Acknowledgments

A few years ago, as I entered my third decade in education and my fifth decade of life, I began to look more closely in the rearview mirror. I reflected on where I came from in my own education, where I started my career in education, and where my next career steps would be. After spending over three decades in education, I took the time to look not only at my scholarship, but also at my work as a junior high teacher, high school administrator, faculty member, and colleague. *Dispositions Are a Teacher's Greatest Strength: Mindful Pedagogical Practices to Develop Self-Awareness to Flourish in the Classroom* is the culmination of my recent reflections and collective career from my first days as a junior high English teacher to my final days of teaching at the college. I am grateful to have worked in both public and private school environments, and I sincerely appreciate the opportunity to serve and develop my skills in a stimulating and challenging profession.

I spent over a year writing *Dispositions Are a Teacher's Greatest Strength* while working, teaching, and supervising student teachers. In Summer 2023, after the academic year ended, I was eager for a road trip to the mountains where I could rest and hike with family, and finish writing this book. Instead, I found myself writing at my parents' house, 2500 hundred miles away from my home on the west coast. Rather than resting, hiking, and writing, I was living with and helping my parents after my dad had an extensive surgery. In place of writing in the mountains, I sat at my parents' dining room table and wrote for several months, regularly jumping up to help my dad in recovery. During this challenging season, I dug deep and found surprising dispositional strength to write, as well as to support, listen to, and help my dad heal. While writing and editing, I unexpectedly acknowledged each disposition in this book, its significance, and strength that I needed under the unique circumstances. I realized that as I've prioritized dispositions in my professional life and scholarship, the self-awareness and skills I've nurtured over time overflowed into my personal life. We often hear that it is hard for teachers to separate their teacher persona from their individual persona outside of the classroom. This past summer, I found this to be the case as I recognized each of the book's 13 dispositions evolving in myself. And thankfully, I did finally take a road trip to the mountains to put the finishing touches on the book.

I chose each disposition for *Dispositions Are a Teacher's Greatest Strength* with gratitude and acknowledgment of my years of experience in the field. Whether I was serving in administration, teaching undergraduate courses, observing a student teacher, or giving a junior high spelling test, each disposition played and continues to play a role in my professional life as well as in the lives of my educator colleagues and friends. Intentionally pursuing dispositions in my work, as well as sharing them, has fueled me and reminded me of my purpose and commitment to the profession. Connecting the dots between a teacher's head and heart skills—while also working to grow and strengthen each of this book's 13 dispositions—reminds me of my calling to teach as well as the joys and challenges I've experienced throughout my career.

As this book goes to print, I feel great gratitude for the encouragement and guidance of my editor at Routledge/ Taylor and Francis Group, Emmie Shand. I am also thankful for Prabhu Chinnasamy and the team of copyeditors, designers, and typesetters who helped bring this book to life.

I extend additional appreciation to my former student and friend, Shae, who has been a consistent sounding board, brainstorming partner, research assistant, and editor. Shae helped me with the proposal and read every word of this book several times. I am also grateful to my new friend, Jamie, who found weeks of time to offer editing expertise and suggestions to strengthen *Dispositions Are a Teacher's Greatest Strength*.

My colleagues and friends at Westmont College, specifically those in the Education Department, enthusiastically supported my vision and work with dispositions through the years. I am forever grateful. From my first days as a graduate student to my final days at the college, thank you for the support. I also appreciate my dear friend and mentor Ken, who encouraged me years ago in graduate school and has since guided me through the proposal and book writing process. I continue to learn so much from you, Ken, and I appreciate your consistent investment in me.

As always, I am thankful for "Team Michelle," my amazing village of friends and family, who ask about my writing and cheer for me along the way. You know who you are! My extended family also deserves a round of applause for their consistent support and love. To my husband Chris, and my grown-up children, Haley and Grant, I love you and appreciate your high fives, hugs, and interest in what I do; you inspire me every day to do and be better.

I extend additional thanks to all my students who have taught me, inspired me, and encouraged me through the years. You are *the why* to my work and writing. You make a challenging day better and you make the work worthwhile. Thank you for supporting me and for embracing the dispositions I hold dear.

And finally, to every educator who chooses to read *Dispositions Are a Teacher's Greatest Strength*, I hope the words on these pages nudge you to reflect and care for your heart. May the book give you a warm hug of affirmation for your commitment to learning, students, professional growth, and the teaching profession. Thank you for all you do.

1

Introduction

Why Dispositions?

Why Dispositions?

In everyday life, there are things small and large that jolt us, shift us, and shape us. The COVID-19 pandemic was a major disruption that literally shut down the globe and posed unprecedented challenges for educators. Transitioning to online learning, teachers had little time and space to think about dispositions or developing dispositional habits. Dispositions, the attitudes, postures, and commitments of the heart, took a backseat as schools grappled with responding to the most urgent educational needs. Ironically, after the initial shock and forced transitions to virtual classrooms, many educators found that they were forced to spend time with themselves; unanticipated time for reflection produced greater self-awareness for many teachers even through the painstaking transitions. Educators were pressed to adapt to online learning, increased work demands, limited access to resources, students' learning gaps, and the strain of daily uncertainty. The trauma as well as the isolation deeply affected teachers as the pandemic pushed the aforementioned issues further into the national spotlight. Post-pandemic, there is a critical need to address teachers' humanity and self-care, while not forgetting teachers' ongoing service on the frontlines. At the same

DOI: 10.4324/9781003379539-1

time, because of new stressors and pressures produced during the pandemic, pre-service and seasoned teachers may be lacking dispositional effectiveness more than ever before; educators' mental health and dispositional endurance are areas in need of immediate attention.

Dispositions and Self-care

Researching dispositional development has been the priority and joy of my scholarship for the last 15 years; *Dispositions Are a Teacher's Greatest Strength* serves as the culmination of my scholarship. The book takes a practical look at dispositional development as a means for career sustainability. Dispositions can supply teachers with essential tools to face the unexpected curve balls that life throws at us.

Investing time, reflecting on, and discussing dispositions can be employed as a form of self-care. I am not an expert on self-care; however, I believe that taking time to rest and recharge doesn't happen enough for teachers. With increasing demands on a teacher's time, I hope *Dispositions Are a Teacher's Greatest Strength* will motivate educators to make space for self-care and dispositional habits even when their schools do not. Pausing to breathe and think about our values, actions, and responses in the classroom can reap benefits for our students. Medical doctor and author Pooja Lakshmin recognizes that self-care acts as decision-making that weaves through our life choices (2023).

Noting the common human tendency to feel that we are swimming upstream, she encourages small efforts to help prevent burnout (rather than attempting quick fixes). Lakshmin advocates for a professional to do the inner work that reinforces self-care as an intentional practice that takes time, commitment, and routine reflection. In her theory of care, Nel Noddings argues that there is a human need to receive and offer care (2003). Her theory is essential for the teacher and student relationship. One of my education colleagues has spent extensive time researching educational care; he notes in a recent study that teacher-caring intentions and actions do not always transfer to students because there can be a disconnect between student experiences, student perceptions, teacher actions, and teacher intentions (Schat, 2021). In his research, Sean Schat examines 13 distinct categories of teacher behavior. These behaviors influence the communication of care. Of particular significance, teacher actions that focus on student well-being and mental health are a means of offering care; in other words, it isn't enough to offer an action of care until the student recognizes the care and responds to the care. This is an important point to consider as we explore the role of dispositions in the classroom because, according to Schat, every aspect of teaching involves care communication. After learning this, I became curious about how and when teachers take time to care for themselves and their colleagues.

Prioritizing self-care, whether by finding more time to exercise, sleep, or gather with friends, reaps benefits; and because teachers look out for their students' well-being, self-care is essential for professional flourishing (Hollabaugh & Ballance, 2022). Similarly, the book *Self Care for Educators, Soul-Nourishing Practices to Promote Wellbeing* takes a holistic look at soul-nourishing practices post-pandemic (Freytag & Shotsberger, 2022). The book's authors promote teacher nourishment—nourishment of the physical self, cognitive self, emotional self, and spiritual self as healthy self-care. Self-care is essentially an unselfish act that fosters personal well-being, promotes renewal, and fights burnout. Elena Aguilar's research also recognizes that self-acceptance and self-love strengthen our resilience (2018).

As I mentioned earlier, teachers often put others before themselves. The emotional toll of teaching and its impact on educators (even pre-pandemic) continues to be an ongoing concern. Educators often find it difficult to discuss their own vulnerabilities, and as a result, they neglect their own care. Teachers may not take the time, or they may not be provided the time in the workplace, to pause and reflect to consider what they need. Additionally, teacher burnout and falling teacher retention rates remain alarming, reinforcing the call to prioritize teacher wellness to improve retention. Equipping and encouraging teachers to destress and implement self-care can help prevent burnout. Self-directed strategies, such as mindful breath work, stretching, daily time for pause, and accountability colleagues, are practical methods to consider when addressing teachers' wellness. With much of the country's mental health focus on students, advocating for increased attention on practical tools to proactively sustain teachers in the profession is needed (Liebenow & Philibert, 2022). Teaching will continue to be a challenging profession; yet if novice teachers are equipped with self-care tools and practices, they have a better chance of thriving in their work (Hollabaugh & Ballance, 2022, p. 131). Because of this, I challenge educators, new to the field and those that are decades into their teaching careers, to explore dispositions as part of a self-care routine for continued professional learning and growth.

Exploring Dispositions

Teaching is commonly characterized as a calling—motivation, talent, and life experience are often part of an individual's sense of calling as a teacher. In recent years, teaching has become a job that many educators find harder to love; frequently framed as a self-less calling, teaching can at times feel unsustainable. More than ever before, teachers must function as therapists and mental health workers, safety consultants, and snack providers. I believe that developing dispositions can help us attend to the soft skills or the harder-to-measure skills of the profession. As a point of clarification, the term, *soft skills*, does not suggest that dispositions are less important than traditional pedagogical skills; however, dispositions are often overlooked when a teacher's to-do list is long or their plate is too full.

Teaching, often viewed as not just what you do, but who you are, is a profession that involves dispositions that can preserve and renew a teacher's heart for students and the classroom. Dispositions—such as curiosity, gratitude, and adaptability, to name a few—are not taught in textbooks; yet understandably, dispositions often take a back seat to more urgent classroom responsibilities such as lesson planning, management strategies, and parent conferences that typically consume a teacher's time and energy. I find that dispositions are often disregarded when curriculum, bell schedules, standardized assessments, and grading are prioritized in schools. At the same time, dispositions can and should be linked to pedagogy, curriculum, and essential skills for the classroom because when they are linked to academic skills and theories, dispositions elevate all aspects of a teacher's work and shift the narrative; dispositions, the "core skills and key competencies" (Greene, 2016, p. 33) such as empathy, curiosity, or resilience weave through every facet of a teacher's classroom responsibilities. Additionally, it becomes critical to recognize that habits and behaviors—as well as practicing habits and behaviors—help educators develop dispositions in order to engage in reflective practice and develop self-awareness, share dispositions, and grow professionally (Aguilar, 2018). Some of my earliest research on dispositions revealed that growing one's dispositional awareness creates an increased desire to engage with and infuse dispositions into practice; thus, strengthening our professional practice with dispositions at the forefront adds meaning and value to our work (Hughes, 2014).

Digging into Dispositions

Dispositions are often characterized as the virtues, values, traits, and habits that inform professional actions. As mentioned in the preface, dispositions defined by the Council for the Accreditation of Educator Preparation are the "habits of professional action and moral commitments that underlie an educator's performance" (2016, p. 6). Over the last 15 years, in my work with student teachers and cooperating teachers in the field, I have found that dispositions give teachers a sense of purpose. Dispositions enlarge a teacher's perspective and inform decision-making. They shape our habits and behaviors. Although most of my research is focused on dispositional development specific to pre-service education, I believe developing dispositions in practice applies to all teachers whatever their age or career stage.

Historically, dispositional research, specific to pre-service programs and teacher training, has been limited. Philosopher

John Dewey initially proclaimed that teachers need to be open-minded, reflective, and curious (Dewey, 1906; Meadows, 2012). Dispositions were first added to the standards of the National Council for Accreditation of Teacher Education in the United States in 2000. Soon after, pre-service programs began to consider how to prepare qualified candidates with content knowledge, skills, *and* professional suitability (Honawar, 2008; Manzo, 2006). Additional literature revealed diverse approaches and inconsistent models for dispositions in practice due to the intangible nature of dispositions. Not only are dispositions hard to see and touch but there wasn't a clear universal standard for their assessment (Murrell et al., 2010). In addition, researcher Richard Osguthorpe recognized the significance of dispositions in educational practice as well as the impact of dispositions on the moral dimension of teaching; he also claimed that there was a lack of attention given to the moral and ethical aspects of pre-service education (2013). Over time, dispositional development evolved as an essential dimension of teacher preparation. Subsequent research recommended that pre-service programs shouldn't reduce dispositions to a mere checklist, but instead should develop and assess dispositions throughout teacher training (Mahoney & Ward, 2014; Osguthorpe, 2013). Moreover, balancing effective teacher qualities with best practice, rather than assessing dispositions as a single standardized measurement or evaluative rating, can help teachers understand themselves and flourish (Mahoney & Ward, 2014, p. 179).

Notably, dispositions should not be assessed in isolation from other teacher skills but, instead, should connect to the knowledge, skills, and practice that help teachers translate dispositions into action. Dispositions should be talked about, modeled, and assessed with transparency, whether through conversations, written reflections, or active participation with new or veteran teachers. From pre-service faculty to principals and teachers in K-12, there is a need to understand dispositions, their significance, and the practical ways to nurture them in professional practice. Researching dispositions, I recognize that it is most often up to teachers and individual school leaders to create time and space to develop dispositions even though developing dispositions can serve as a powerful means for teacher growth and self-care for career sustainability.

It is critical to recognize that teaching is a moral enterprise and there are ways teachers can build capacities and acknowledge the dignity and humanity in the profession. Teacher responsibility is anchored in morals and values that can stimulate and motivate teachers to pursue and develop dispositions (Sherman, 2013). In *The Nicomachaen Ethics*, one of Aristotle's most profound works, the esteemed philosopher concluded that moral virtue is formed through actions, habits, and vigilance (Aristotle et al., 2012). For example, if we attentively choose to act and model empathy, we will develop empathy, or if we choose to act and model adaptability, we will develop adaptability. Dispositions lie at the heart of teaching; therefore, building dispositional competency can be an inspirational endeavor. Providing time and space for discourse, application, and reflection can serve as rich opportunities that validate dispositions and their role in the classroom. Teachers need vital support, opportunities to grow, and inspiration as nutrition for career longevity. Moreover, nurturing the competencies of prospective teachers impacts teachers' responsiveness to students and contributes to a teacher's effectiveness (Sherman, 2013).

Experience teaches us and prepares us for the future (Sittser, 2000, p. 170). Educators must find balance to implement both the practical and the theoretical in practice. Pre-service candidates (and veteran teachers) need to observe demonstrated dispositions in clinical settings (Dottin, 2009). Candidates need to explore how they act and react in a variety of contexts. Pre-service programs set the tone for a teacher's future and help guide candidates to think through dispositions, examples in their own practice, and interactions with students and colleagues. One study in particular suggests introducing professional dispositions in pre-service programs through discussion, role play, reflection, and assignments, so that new teachers can begin to recognize the value and benefits of professional dispositions in practice (Dunkle & Ahuna, 2014, p. 202). Pre-service programs need to train teachers to foster relevant dispositions such as reflection, inclusion, and collaboration, so that they carry these habits into their first teaching positions (Hughes, 2014, 2020). I find dispositions, as well as professional standards and ethics, are non-negotiables for maintaining safe, culturally responsive, and just classrooms for students. Dispositions demonstrated in practice also build teachers' awareness and enrich their professional development.

It is important to acknowledge that dispositions are rooted in teachers' cultural backgrounds, lived experiences, and family lives. Teachers are not exempt from or immune to certain behaviors, biases, or presuppositions that can hurt and marginalize students or even colleagues. Attention to dispositions is one way to humanize and empower teachers; however, the way teachers manifest and demonstrate dispositions isn't fixed and may look different from teacher to teacher. Early research on dispositions showed that knowledge, actions, behaviors, and skills can't be separated. They are interrelated—they connect a teacher's head, heart, commitments, knowledge, and skills. Furthermore, as mentioned above, dispositions include a moral and ethical component (Feiman-Nemser & Schussler, 2010). Teachers know that with their work comes a significant moral responsibility. When we discuss moral and ethical teaching, we often think of a moral compass and how it motivates and drives us into action. In this way, creating opportunities for teachers in training to recognize personal biases and misconceptions as well as the influence of their own backgrounds help novice teachers think on their feet, adjust, and respond with dispositional commitment (p. 189). Although teaching is a complex enterprise, teachers can use dispositions as a resource for professional practice. For instance, teaching all learners through a culturally sensitive lens is fundamental to a teacher's practice. Consequently, humanizing dispositions—linking core habits of mind, actions, and heart—is essential to best practice and affirms a teacher's knowledge, actions, and commitments regarding what matters most (Feiman-Nemser & Schussler, 2010, p. 182). With intention and determination, dispositional capacity grows over time. In addition, dispositional awareness generates space for a teacher to not only feel empowered but to also empower and support students. Furthermore, showing our care for students through attitudes and actions that convey hope, gratitude, or joy sends the message that we genuinely value students and are committed to them and their success.

I hope that *Dispositions Are a Teacher's Greatest Strength* will encourage educators to consider how they can identify, foster, and elevate their own dispositional self-awareness. As teachers face increasing professional pressures, focusing on, discussing, and exploring professional teaching dispositions remains an underutilized professional tool. With the "great teacher resignation" post-pandemic, we need to double down on efforts to promote the profession as well as retain the teachers we currently have (Vatterott, 2022). Notably, teachers need dispositions to teach well and live healthy, productive lives.

Choosing the Road to Dispositions

Author John Ortberg suggests that "open-door people" possess an open mindset with a set of habits and practices that help them walk through open doors (2015, p. 25). He recognizes that open-door people are ready for life's challenges and opportunities. Dispositions can help educators venture or adventure through an open door. Similarly, Robert Frost's famous poem, *The Road Not Taken* (2017, p. 87), tells readers about a narrator coming across two merging roads in the woods, choosing the road not taken or the road without wear. The poet notes that choosing the less-trodden path makes all the difference. Each semester, I share this poem with my student teachers to prompt a discussion related to sitting with or dealing with the uncomfortable. I view building dispositional awareness through a lens or a road similar to the road less traveled. In other words, focusing on curriculum, lesson planning, and pedagogy are the traditional and essential roads that most teachers choose; however, Frost's suggested road can be an opportunity to opt for a road with some risk. What's more, understanding ourselves as individuals and professionals' urges digging deep, reflecting routinely, being open to learning and growing, and often looking at ourselves in the mirror. Similar to Frost's poem, many of us have probably seen the illustration of two arrows pointing to success; one arrow is a straight arrow; the other is a curvy arrow; yet, both arrows point to and arrive at success. These arrows, like the poem, can be a metaphor for pursuing dispositions in practice. Dispositions, with attention and effort, can make the difference for teachers; dispositions can uplift teacher practice, sustain teachers, develop teachers, and bring greater meaning to their daily work in the classroom.

As previously noted, since my early graduate school days, I have studied and written about professional teaching dispositions. Subsequently, the pre-service program in which I work adopted four dispositions that align with the Council for the Accreditation of Teacher Education's definition of dispositions (2016): "pre-service students and faculty seek to demonstrate each disposition in credential classes, coursework, and clinical experiences. The four dispositions, *lifelong learner*, *reflective practitioner*, *compassionate professional*, and *grateful servant*, are introduced early in the program and are sustained across the arc of program through assignments, lessons, collegial exchanges, reflections, and self-assessments" (Department of Education Dispositions Statement, 2021, p. 5; Hughes, 2014). Early in our program, faculty present the four dispositions to student teachers. Together with student teachers, we discuss each disposition along with the implicit and explicit ways student teachers can demonstrate each disposition. Faculty are known to pause mid-lesson to name a disposition they are modeling; in addition, student teachers are expected to write about the four dispositions in their weekly reflections and their cumulative assignments. As student teachers reflect upon, write about, and practice each disposition, they develop self-awareness and habits for each disposition.

As habitual postures, dispositions do not simply occur for new or experienced teachers; they must be intentionally practiced. In particular, teachers form habits of thinking when they collect, reflect, and analyze information to make informed decisions for student learning. Beginning in most pre-service programs, reflection and reflective practices are nurtured non-negotiables in teacher practice. Candidates need exposure to a combination of teacher standards, university supports, coursework, clinical experiences, and assessments to develop dispositions and habits of the heart. Such opportunities must be strategically implemented to ultimately inform decision-making and impact student learning throughout a teacher's career (Huang, 2015).

Early research on dispositions tackled the complexity of assessing dispositions with recommendations for intentional opportunities to identify, reflect on, and grow dispositions in practice; in particular, assessments such as case studies, a teaching philosophy, written and oral reflections, classroom management plans, units of study, or a final portfolio can serve as welcome opportunities for novice teachers to develop dispositions. Each of these assessments, if explicitly linked and unpacked with thoughts and actions, becomes a tool for dispositional development. Furthermore, translating dispositions into actions and responses can strengthen teacher practice (Feiman-Nemser & Schussler, 2010). Teachers, whether in K-12 or higher education, teach and model for students; when their students observe a teacher demonstrating dispositions, the observation impacts students' own dispositional development, habits, and behaviors (Tomlinson, 2015). Educator Carol Ann Tomlinson concludes that dispositional modeling is essential to develop students' hearts and values for inside and outside the classroom. Focusing on dispositions can be a meaningful method to develop not only our professional hearts and minds, but also our students' hearts and minds. As one of my student teachers once said, "Teachers need to be ready to pass on the [dispositional] passion!"

Dispositions Humanize Teachers and Shape Practice

We often hear that teachers have superpowers or that they are superheroes. They are not. Teachers are human. At the same, time, we can't ignore that teachers are known to create wonder, joy, and discovery. For instance, teachers work a type of magic in the classroom when they sit on the floor with students and read theatrically, demonstrate a powerful science experiment, or connect a hands-on field trip to a classroom text. Simply tapping into a love for subject matter and the ebb and flow of the school year can cultivate moments of classroom magic. Although dispositions can be a secret source of inner strength for teachers, I do not want to perpetuate the misconception or expectation that teachers should somehow be super-human. Instead, I suggest that maintaining a focus on dispositions creates genuine opportunity to develop, humanize, and strengthen what teachers do day in and day out.

Author David Brooks frames openheartedness, a desire to grow personally and professionally, as a qualification to be more fully human (2023). In my experience, when we take time to examine dispositions like celebration, joy, or inclusion, we grow our self-awareness, our heart skills, and our perspective. With 13 hand-picked dispositions, this book invites readers to create space for dispositional development in their busy lives. I genuinely hope reading *Dispositions Are a Teacher's Greatest Strength* will help educators sharpen the postures, values, and beliefs that humanize them in their teaching positions—with encouragement and affirmation.

I would be remiss to not mention that there are dispositions that harm, such as apathy, bitterness, or impatience. Although recognizing harmful dispositions within ourselves can benefit educators in thoughtful ways, I believe the dispositions explored in this book enrich and deepen teacher practice in proactive ways. Subsequently, I intentionally chose dispositions that support teacher assets rather than teacher deficits. Teaching is heart, mind, and soul work. *Dispositions Are a Teacher's Greatest Strength* can remind teachers of the meaningful work in our profession and put dispositions at the forefront of our classrooms. This book serves as validation for the challenges teaching presents as well as invites teachers everywhere to ponder and constructively engage with distinct dispositions that honor our chosen profession and the work it requires.

One of my graduate school professors once shared that teachers have so much to offer—well beyond being in charge of curriculum and classroom management; teachers offer and share their humanity with others. Hence, my fundamental desire for this book is for teachers to cultivate fresh perspective and energy, as well as provide opportunity to grow both professionally and personally. With practical strategies, classroom anecdotes, and relevant research, this book can be used to foster dispositional growth. I offer *Dispositions Are a Teacher's Greatest Strength* as a humble invitation, an opportunity, to engage intentionally with 13 core dispositions.

When considering dispositions, it is worth taking a moment to consider self-efficacy theory (Bandura, 1997). This theory is important to a teacher's dispositional work because teachers know that students show up to school with their own self-image and competencies that are shaped by their parents, siblings, friends, and culture. Others' beliefs also influence a student's (and a teacher's) convictions as well as their motivation. A teacher's influence and ability to care for students and invest in students' self-efficacy, agency, and confidence is pivotal to student development. The classroom provides rich context and opportunity for teachers to model, share, and demonstrate dispositions to students to help shape their thinking and character.

Teachers have the gift of consistency and time in a given school year, Monday through Friday. Much like when teachers consider students' multiple intelligences, teachers must thoughtfully consider the dispositions they possess as well as those that their students possess. Students and teachers are not born with all of the dispositions explored in *Dispositions Are a Teacher's Greatest Strength*; however, dispositions do develop over time with experience, intention, and practice. Focusing on teacher qualities takes a comprehensive approach that includes both the heart and mind (Day, 2004; Tomlinson, 2015). Michael Epstein, a medical doctor from the University of Rochester, emphasizes that there is a need in medicine to develop habits of mind for the doctor's office, operating room, and medical clinic (2003). He argues that textbooks, rules, and clear instructions are important in the medical practice, but individual doctors must also arm themselves with skills to adapt, develop new knowledge, and strengthen performance. Epstein promotes engaging in reflection and mindfulness with medical students just like pre-service faculty and supervisors do with student teachers and principals do with their teaching staffs. Doctors care for their patients, and likewise, teachers care for their students; dispositional habits benefit professionals in both contexts.

What to Expect While Reading?

As part of my professional practice and by design, I have researched a new disposition each year; choosing to do this has poignantly sparked a renewed sense of energy and hope in me. Each chapter in this book contains definition and context for a disposition of focus. Each chapter also includes practical application to practice and develop dispositions, such as resilience, empathy, and collaboration, offering practical examples for teachers to cultivate each disposition. In addition, the conclusion of each chapter presents a set of questions for reflection so that teachers can "pause and reflect." I hope teacher-readers will move from simply reading about a specific disposition to contemplating how they can identify, develop, and grow more deeply into each disposition.

While there are a multitude of dispositions I could write about; I chose to focus on 13 core dispositions. Each disposition was intentionally selected and scaffolded in a particular order; for instance, I placed Chapter 3 on reflection at the start of the book because reflection seems to connect to every other disposition in the book in some way. I placed Chapter 12 on hope later in the book—with the intention to uplift, elevate, and even help heal an educator's worn-out heart. Each chapter's dispositional focus is rooted with anticipation of providing opportunities for educators to ponder contexts that can inspire dispositional growth in themselves and their students. As previously mentioned, several of the dispositions in this book are prioritized in the preservice program where I teach. I chose to focus on two additional dispositions, resilience and hope, in response to several natural disasters and disruptions in my own community. And I chose six more dispositions that I consider to be pre-requisite postures needed by teachers. I don't know everything there is to know about dispositions, but through study and experience, I am certain the dispositions in this book will contribute to teacher flourishing. Exploring and reflecting on dispositions, individually or collectively, is worth the time and investment. I sincerely hope that as educators read *Dispositions Are a Teacher's Greatest Strength*, they feel encouraged and even share their discoveries with students and colleagues; this book can be read individually, with a book club, in a pre-service preparation course, or through a school's professional development training.

Dispositions Strengthen a Teacher's Heart

Understanding ourselves as teaching professionals means we choose to be vulnerable, to reflect, and to seek to understand ourselves and each other. Author Brené Brown believes that vulnerability is the starting place for identifying our purpose—for finding meaning, hope, and clarity (2012; 2018). Vulnerability translates to finding courage to know ourselves, be ourselves, and strive to grow. Being open and vulnerable with ourselves nurtures growth and a greater ability to connect with others. We demonstrate strength when we engage in vulnerability with others (Mackesy, 2023); and our vulnerability gives others permission to share about themselves (Aguilar, 2018). Of course, there is a time and a place for vulnerability both with ourselves and with our students. The recently popularized term "oversharer" characterizes a person who shares too many personal details or doesn't have boundaries with their thoughts and opinions. When I consider dispositions, I am not focused on this type of vulnerability; instead, I hope to welcome and embrace opportunities for vulnerability in order to develop alongside students and colleagues. Might we take advantage of times to share stories of struggle, talk about tenacity, and process with others? Might we get more mileage or "bang for our buck" with students and colleagues during moments of vulnerability and authenticity?

Early in my teaching career, I remember a principal saying to me, "Don't let them [the students] see you cry." I took this instruction to mean that no matter what the circumstance, I should never allow students to see my tears. Through the years, as I matured professionally, I allowed my students see me cry at what I felt were appropriate moments. For example, when a student lost a loved one, or when my school community had a student pass away, my shared tears felt appropriate. I have also shed tears with student teachers when we have discussed school safety or horrifying school shootings. Some of the most meaningful moments in my career have been when I have cried with a student teacher when something hasn't gone well for them or when I needed to challenge a student teacher to elevate their preparation or presence. This type of vulnerability, when shared sincerely and without agenda, feels appropriate. Sharing our vulnerability can bring greater meaning to our work and relationships. In addition, vulnerability and mistake-making are becoming more of the accepted norms in classrooms. In his book, *Teach Like a Champion* (2021), Doug Lemov proposes that teachers must create classrooms where students feel safe to make mistakes. These classroom contexts are spaces where errors are the norm and mistake-making becomes part of the learning process. Responding to students with statements such as "That was really hard, but I appreciate your tenacity" or "I appreciate that you took a risk and tried. You are growing!" highlights Lemov's approach. Furthermore, sharing professional vulnerability when we make mistakes as teachers, either with students or with colleagues, remains a valuable strategy that conveys our love for learning, our commitment to the learning process, and our authenticity.

Dispositions Are a Teacher's Greatest Strength is written for all educators—for teachers, administrators, pre-service candidates, higher education faculty, and school communities—who want to strengthen practices of the heart. The book is an invitation to consider how to teach in empowering ways and consider the potential of growing dispositions in practice. My sincere hope is that through the research, strategies, and reflection opportunities highlighted throughout the book, teachers will feel encouraged. Developing and exercising our dispositional muscles can help us thoughtfully care for our students as well as our own teacher-hearts. I confidently urge you to invest in your dispositional development alongside the to-do lists of your classroom because teaching is an ongoing journey that develops and shapes our craft as well as who we are as individuals and professionals (Paris, 2016). I once heard someone proclaim that teachers need to give a high five to their hearts. Taking the time to nurture dispositions can do just that. As you turn the page and keep reading, I am sending a few high fives your way.

Pause and Reflect

1. After reading this chapter in *Dispositions Are a Greatest Strength*, which dispositions spark your curiosity and why?
2. Consider how much time and space you've been given in your professional life to ponder, embrace, and strengthen dispositions in practice? How does this make you feel?
3. How might dispositions such as adaptability, courage, and gratitude enrich your professional practice?
4. In what specific ways have you neglected your own self-care? What specific changes can you make to renew your own self-care efforts?
5. Ponder a time when you have felt invigorated professionally. What steps can you take to feel this way again?

References

Aguilar, E. (2018). *Onward: Cultivating emotional resilience in educators.* Jossey-Bass.

Aristotle, Bartlett, R. C., & Collins, S. D. (2012). *Artistotle's nicomachaene ethics.* University of Chicago Press.

Bandura (1997). *Self-efficacy: The exercise of control.* Worth Publishers.

Brooks, D. (2023). The essential skills for being human. *The New York Times.* https://www.nytimes.com/2023/10/19/opinion/social-skills-connection.html?searchResultPosition=1

Brown, B. (2012). *Daring greatly: How the courage to be vulnerable transforms the way we love, parent, and lead.* Avery.

Brown, B. (2018). *Dare to lead. Brave work. Tough conversations. Whole hearts.* Random House.

Council for the Accreditation of Educator Preparation (2016). In TASC model core teaching standards (p. 6). https://caepnet.org/glossary?letter=D

Day, C. (2004). *A passion for teaching.* Routledge.

Department of Education Dispositions Statement (2021). In *Westmont Department of Education Teacher Credential Program Handbook 2022-2023*, p. 5. https://www.westmont.edu/sites/default/files/users/user451/Teacher%20Credential%20Handbook%20for%20Printing_0.pdf

Dewey, J. (1906). *The child and the curriculum.* University of Chicago Press.

Dottin, E. S. (2009). Professional judgment and dispositions in teacher education. *Teaching and Teacher Education, 25*(1), 83–88. https://doi.org/10.1016/j.tate.2008.06.005

Dunkle, S. M., & Ahuna, K. H. (2014). Professional dispositions for teacher candidates. In J. A. Gorlewski, D. A. Gorlewski, J. Hopkins, & Porfilio, B. J. (Eds.), *Effective or wise?* (pp. 197–211). Peter Lang.

Epstein, R. M. (2003). Mindful practice in action (II): Cultivating habits of mind. *Families, Systems, & Health, 21*(1), 11–17. https://doi.org/10.1037/h0089495

Feiman-Nemser, S., & Schussler, D. L. (2010). Defining, developing, and assessing dispositions: A cross-case analysis. In P. C. Murrell, M. E. Diez, S. Feiman-Nemser, & D. L. Schussler (Eds.), *Teaching as a moral practice* (pp. 177–201). Harvard Education Press.

Freytag, C. E., & Shotsberger, P. (2022). *Self care for educators: Soul nourishing practices to promote wellbeing.* Freedom's Hill Press.

Frost, R. (2017). *The road not taken and other poems.* Digireads.com Publishing.

Greene, J. (2016). Soft skills: Preparing kids for life after school. *Association for Middle Level Education Magazine, 5*(1), 33–34. https://www.amle.org/soft-skills-preparing-kids-for-life-after-school/

Hollabaugh, J., & Ballance, M. (2022). Self care for novice teachers. In C. E. Freytag, & P. Shotsberger (Eds.), *Self care for educators* (pp. 112–138). Freedom's Hill Press.

Honawar, V. (2008). Teacher education community is striving to inter-
pret candidate 'dispositions'. Education Week. https://www.
edweek.org/policy-politics/teacher-ed-community-is-striving-to-
interpret-candidate-dispositions/2008/03

Huang, J. L. (2015). Cultivating teacher-thinking: Ideas and practice,
Educational Research for Policy and Practice, 14, 247–257. https://
doi.org/10.1007/s10671-015-9184-1

Hughes, M. C. (2014). One pre-service program's dispositional efforts
revealed. [Doctoral dissertation, George Fox University]. Digital
Commons at George Fox University.

Hughes, M. C. (2020). Dispositions: Real time active practice. In P.
Shotsberger, & C. E. Freytag (Eds.), *How shall we then care? A Christian
educator's guide for caring for self, learners, colleagues, and community* (pp. 137–158). Wipf and Stock.

Lakshmin, P. (2023) *Real self-care: A transformative program for redefining
wellness. Penguin Life.*

Lemov, D. (2021). *Teach like a champion 3.0.* Jossey-Bass.

Liebenow, P., & Philibert, C. T. (2022). Two tracks toward wellness:
Address students' and teachers' mental health with a two-pronged
strategy. *Principal, 102*(1), 22–25. https://www.naesp.org/resource/
two-tracks-toward-wellness/

Mackesy, C. (2023). An old drawing [Highlight]. Instagram https://www.
instagram.com/charliemackesy/

Mahoney, T., & Ward, J. (2014). Seeking balance: Rethinking who decides
the role of teacher of dispositions in teacher evaluation. In J. A.
Gorlewski, D. A. Gorlewski, J. Hopkins, & B. J. Porfilio (Eds.), *Effective
or wise?* (pp. 177–196). Peter Lang.

Manzo, K. K. (2006). Teacher-hopeful runs afoul of 'dispositions'. Education
Week. https://www.edweek.org/teaching-learning/teacher-hopeful-
runs-afoul-of-dispositions/2006/01

Meadows, E. (2012). Preparing teachers to be curious, open-minded
and reflective: Dewey's ideas reconsidered. *Action in Teacher
Education, 28*(2), 11–14.

Murrell, P. C., Diez, M. E., Feiman-Nemser, S., & Schussler, D. L. (2010).
Teaching as a moral practice. Harvard Press.

Noddings, N. (2003). *Caring: A feminine approach to ethics and moral
education* (2nd ed.). University of California Press.

Ortberg, J. (2015). *All the places to go: How will you know?* Tyndale House.

Osguthorpe, R. D. (2013). Attending to ethical and moral dispositions in teacher education. *Issues in Teacher Education 22*(1), 17–28. https://files.eric.ed.gov/fulltext/EJ1013927.pdf

Paris, J. (2016). *Teach from the heart: Pedagogy as spiritual practice.* Cascade/Wipf and Stock.

Schat, S. J. (2021). Exploring student experiences of teacher care communication: The offering of educational care. *Pastoral Care in Education: An International Journal of Personal. Social and Emotional Development, 41*(1), 4–25. https://doi.org/10.1080/02643944.2021.1999311

Sherman, S. C. (2013). *Teacher preparation as an inspirational practice: Building capacities for responsiveness.* Routledge.

Sittser, J. (2000). *The will of God as a way of life: How to make every decision with peace and confidence.* Zondervan.

Tomlinson, C. A. (2015). Being human in the classroom. *Educational Leadership, 73*(2), 74–77. https://www.ascd.org/el/articles/being-human-in-the-classroom

Vatterott, C. (2022). Lessons on student well-being from the great resignation. *Educational Leadership, 79*(9). https://www.ascd.org/el/articles/lessons-on-student-well-being-from-the-great-resignation

2

Curiosity

Curiosity Defined

"Class, I stayed up so late last night because I couldn't stop watching a fascinating documentary on dolphins!" This statement, shared with great enthusiasm, conveys curiosity in a simple yet tangible way. In an ideal classroom, both students and teachers share and demonstrate a spirit of inquiry for learning. Teachers strive to inspire students in creative ways when they model curiosity, intrigue, and a love for learning in novel ways so that students become unique "fellow travelers in search of some small glimpse of the truth" (Bain, 2004, p. 143). Yet, how do teachers develop and demonstrate curiosity?

Merriam–Webster defines curiosity as a noun: "a desire to know" or "an interest that leads to inquiry" (2023). A team of researchers frames curiosity as a function of personality whereby humans seek information and the novelty of finding new information (Zurn & Bassett, 2018). They acknowledge the challenge in finding a universal definition for curiosity because information seeking can take different forms as the brain develops. Additionally, understanding the psychology of curiosity can steer educators toward greater curiosity and motivate students to search for information (Pluck & Johnson, 2011). Because curiosity is fundamental to human cognition (Kidd & Hayden, 2015) and because of increased brain research, there is a fresh focus on the psychology of curiosity. Curiosity envelops a basic

DOI: 10.4324/9781003379539-2

desire for information or stimulation *and* intrinsic and extrinsic motivation point to the benefits of curiosity—both immediate and long-term—for enriched learning. Examining, inquiring, probing, and wondering about topics and information reveal curiosity; seeking new information exposes this unique disposition. Furthermore, inquiry-based learning, regular feedback, and assessments of knowledge are distinct instructional approaches that can uniquely connect the dots between curiosity and learning (Pluck & Johnson, 2011).

Thanks to the immediacy of technology with the internet, iPhones, laptop computers, and most recently, Artificial Intelligence or AI, humans are conditioned to look up what they don't know. We ask Siri or Alexa about word spellings and definitions, the weather forecast, and driving directions. Although these examples don't feel very academic, they do show how individuals act on their curiosity and desires to find out new information, albeit effortlessly. As an educator, I wonder (note that I just modeled curiosity with the use of the statement *I wonder*) if teachers should make a distinction between a student's genuine curiosity and quest for new knowledge versus our current culture's urgency to Google something in the moment. Technology is often all-consuming as our wonderings are quickly appeased with immediate and timely answers. In full transparency, I must admit that most of the time, I take a more traditional approach (sorry Siri and Alexa) to developing and modeling curiosity in practice. Although technology plays a key role in present-day classrooms, contemplating when and how teachers demonstrate curiosity, as professionals (and as humans), is where I focused my energy in this chapter.

Conduits to Curiosity

Not surprisingly, children that are more curious have increased academic outcomes, increased motivation, and more positive social outcomes (Audet & Jordan, 2005). In addition, asking questions to ignite and build cognitive interest can impact student achievement in positive ways (Goodwin, 2022). So, how might a teacher model their love of learning and discovery? As I mentioned in Chapter 1, my colleagues and I view our future teachers as lifelong learners who "display curiosity and passion for learning *and* strive to transfer curiosity to others" (Department of Education Dispositions Statement, 2021, p. 5). We expect student teachers to develop and display a curious spirit and desire to cultivate curiosity. We expect the same of ourselves with the intention of making curiosity contagious. We purposely model how to ask questions that inspire a spirit of investigation and exploration. We also ask student teachers how they can convey curiosity to their own students. I routinely stop class to point out a question or action that demonstrates curiosity. For example, I might ask, "How do you know that?", or I might state, "I wonder why that happened." I also might pause, place an inquisitive look on my face, and say, "Hmmmmm." Intentionally, modeling curiosity extends student thinking and makes curiosity visible. With a curious mindset, knowledge can be like hidden treasure that is worth slowing ourselves down and searching for. As we search for new understanding, new ideas, knowledge, or treasure, educators can grow professionally and share enthusiasm for learning with students.

In order to understand curiosity as part of teacher practice, it is important to ask novice and veteran teachers to describe specifically how they share curiosity with their students. For example, a teacher might say, "I want to learn more about exercise science," or "I have questions about how airplanes get off the ground." Demonstrating curiosity can also come in the form of a statement: "I don't understand, but I want to understand." Teachers and students alike can demonstrate their interest in new ideas when they go to the library to choose a book that sparks interest in a particular topic. They can also display a curious spirit when they look for multiple strategies to solve a math problem. Just as teachers intentionally create space for science exploration, or a Socratic seminar, they must also create space for wonder, investigation, and exploration. Providing time and space for students to stretch their brains can stimulate wonder and awe. Kobi Yamada's children's book *What Do You Do with An Idea?* (2013) highlights the benefits of possessing a curious spirit.

Yamada's book tells the story of a child who has an idea. Because the child gives his idea space to develop, the child begins to see the world differently. Yamada invites his readers to consider curiosity, in the form of an idea, as a means to gain new knowledge and perspective.

Wondering, questioning, and marveling are a professional art. Intentionally asking questions, seeking answers, trying to make sense of the world, people, or things is truly beautiful. When I take time to pause and notice a colleague's curious nature, it feels like a gift—many of my faculty colleagues' model curiosity in wonderful ways through their scholarship, conversations, and teaching. For instance, my colleague Anne (a pseudonym) often takes on the challenge of teaching new courses. Sometimes, this choice is out of necessity, but many times, it is because she is naturally curious. Where many colleagues might rather repeat teaching a course to refine it, Anne truly appreciates the challenge that comes when she dives into developing a new course. Another colleague, Jeffrey (a pseudonym), often wanders into my office to ask me about assessment practices. I so appreciate Jeffrey's spirit of inquiry and desire not only to consider new ideas but to welcome them. Another colleague often says, "Yes, I'll try that," or "I'll research that." She holds an attitude of expectation to learn and a desire to want to problem solve for her department, faculty, and the college as a whole. Her willingness to anticipate and seek new information is a tangible demonstration of inquiry that inspires my own curiosity. Likewise, when I see student teachers get excited about curriculum, I feel invigorated. I find that planning and researching content, and pondering how to make content accessible and stimulating, feels refreshing. It is motivating to hear a student teacher say, "I need to figure out how to engage my students as we study the Korean War," or "I want to read more about strategic grouping for my next unit." I genuinely love the feeling that I have when student teachers make these statements. Likewise, I remember Janelle (a pseudonym), a student teacher who had a handful of challenging students in her art class. Rather than give up on her students, Janelle would often say, "I love this challenge," or "I can't wait to find out more about my students so I can meet their needs." Janelle consistently embraced her students with a spirit of curiosity and a can-do attitude. She was, and is to this day, a problem solver who doesn't accept the status quo at her school; she doesn't let herself get frustrated or discouraged by a student's lack of motivation or behavior challenges. Instead, Janelle models an openness to learn about and support her students with great curiosity. I envy her inquisitive attitude and curious posture in all the best ways.

Scholarship and Curiosity

When I see the many ways and spaces where my colleagues and students demonstrate curiosity, I find that my own writing and scholarship create fertile context, as well as an invitation, for curiosity. Even as I write this chapter, I find that I am posing questions to strengthen my writing and understanding. My natural wonderings frequently turn into specific actions; actions require me to put words down on the page as well as lead me to seek research and resources that will support my work and questions. Possessing a posture of curiosity is stimulating; like the rush of delight teachers feel when a student has an "ah-ha" moment, curiosity energizes and invigorates me professionally.

Diving deeper into the disposition of curiosity, I recall a professional experience that gave me increased understanding of the disposition. I was invited to give a plenary talk at a conference. I felt the professional weight and responsibility of giving the talk; it was called an "Emerging Scholars Talk" and soon after accepting the invitation, I thought about my audience and my messaging. I wondered what I could share that would encourage colleagues in their scholarship. I curiously pondered the notion of emerging which reminded me of my course and assignment rubrics where I often list *emerging* as a category: a student is working toward an expected benchmark, standard, or outcome, but they are not quite there yet. Pre-conference, I was curious about whether my audience and I actually perceive ourselves as a community of emerging professionals and scholars. A quick search of *emerging* on Google Images revealed graphics of lightbulbs, seedlings, rose buds and blooms, cracking eggs, and butterflies. Seeing these images gave me greater clarity regarding growing, learning, and emerging with scholarly purpose. In this instance, my curious spirit helped me write the talk as well as recognize that my scholarly journey is a work in progress that is not yet finished. In light of the disposition of curiosity, emergence taught me that when I think and reflect, I create space for inquiry so that curiosity can flourish. When teachers create space for reflection, they also create space for self-awareness and new knowledge to emerge and stimulate growth. It is ironic that even though educators know this, we need to intentionally find time to give ourselves permission to think, reflect, and cultivate curiosity.

Curiosity and Motivation

Curiosity is fundamental to capturing student attention and can be stimulated by both intrinsic and extrinsic motivation; however, research favors intrinsic motivation for lifelong learning and even future job satisfaction (Day, 2004; Wilson, 2010). When students are given learning opportunities to make choices, learning improves. As a result, students often feel increased competence, a greater sense of control, and a sense that learning is fun. Additionally, curiosity links the enjoyment for learning *and* the challenge of learning that enhances the learning experience. Specifically, when teachers point out the unexpected with surprising aspects or snippets of content, they promote student curiosity (Wilson, 2010).

According to researcher Andrew Hargreaves, educators can create conditions to foster a student's desire to learn with "choice and voice" (2021, p. 41). Hargreaves recommends giving students collaborative experiences, presenting stimulating instruction, being a warm demander, and creating partnerships with families for increased student engagement and motivation. Affirming this thinking, educator Bryan Goodwin suggests that educators also connect learning and content to student interests with hands-on relevant activities (2022). Investing in students, seeing their potential, and fostering skills that prepare them for the common good motivates students *and* inspires educators (Ballock, 2020). Moreover, sharing our professional passions and energy can stimulate not only student curiosity but also our own curiosity and enthusiasm for learning.

A recent *New York Times* essay identified that the key to success, for college students in particular, is possessing an openness to learning and new knowledge (Malesic, 2023). Cultivating curiosity with an appetite for learning can be a valuable approach to grow our brains, our knowledge base, and our perspectives (Griffiths, 2009). Diving into deeper learning or the variety of skills, competencies and dispositions that prepare students to succeed academically can fuel curiosity, creativity, and improved learning. Interdisciplinary content and hands-on projects can also be used to promote increased curiosity for learning (Anderman & Martinez Calvit, 2022).

It is important to point out that standardized testing and other assessments can negatively influence and even squash student curiosity (Audet & Jordan, 2005). Because of this, school leader Jennifer Gallagher advocates for less standardization in education so there can be more curricular creativity, teacher agency, and student agency to develop the innate curiosity that students possess (2023). Simply possessing a desire and an interest in learning for the sake of learning might serve as an antidote for the aforementioned standardization and cultural norms. Thus, promoting academic success that requires postures and habits of genuine curiosity or a desire to know appears to be a noble cause.

Creating Classroom Conditions for Curiosity

Years ago, philosopher John Dewey identified the significance of offering resources, believing in students, and creating learning experiences that foster student growth and progress (Dewey, 1906, 1938; Meadows, 2006). He promoted the idea that students need to actively engage in the process of searching for answers to questions. Creating conditions to inspire student curiosity thoughtfully conveys to students that curiosity is valued and so is student thinking. Dewey repeatedly called educators to stimulate student curiosity by connecting content to student interests; finding ways to capitalize on students' interest nurtures curiosity. Linking lessons to students' interests fosters curiosity whether they are interested in music, soccer, video games, environmental issues, or cooking. As is true with most dispositions, when we get to know our students and when we believe in them, they are more open to learning and growing. Furthermore, when educators intentionally focus on dispositions like curiosity, they raise the bar for student learning.

Similar to other dispositions, curiosity can be contagious. If you've ever seen a group of students get excited about a research topic or group project, you know that the exchanges are joyful to observe and are invigorating for both students and teachers. Meeting students where they are, and identifying and tapping into their interests pay dividends. In addition, I find that when I intentionally nurture curiosity in my students, curiosity stirs in me. I remember many times during discussions or individual meetings with students when I was asked a question that I couldn't answer. In these circumstances, I informed students that I didn't know the answer *yet*, but I would go look for the answer—sometimes the student and I might even choose to search for the answer together. These instances bring about a rush of adrenaline because together, my students and I engage in the treasure-seeking thrill of curiosity.

Curiosity often generates a sense of awe, promotes exploration, and fuels excitement for learning. As we consider how to demonstrate and transfer curiosity to our students, how might we motivate our own hearts and minds toward curiosity? One of my mentors, Ken Badley, offers the image of sweeping students into wonder as we teach content and even as we express wonder ourselves. Presenting opportunities for curiosity and wonder with explicit invitation to wonder creates space for student curiosity and also ensures that students know what stimulates their own thinking (2012). For instance, wondering how chemicals, when mixed together, react or transform can trigger student curiosity. Creating conditions in the classroom that welcome this type of inquiry further taps into a student's curiosity. Curiosity can be a powerful tool for sense making and problem solving; with the proper contexts, curiosity can add perspective and help students understand the world and others (Joseph, 2022). Making sure to demonstrate curiosity with humility, rather than displaying an all-knowing attitude, inspires students' curiosity as they make sense of the world. I resonate with author David Brooks who characterizes curious individuals as illuminators. Brooks recognizes curious people as those who ask questions, desire to learn from and care for others, and want others to feel brighter and larger (2023).

Interestingly, Information Gap Theory suggests that people are most curious when they become aware of small or large gaps in their knowledge. As a result, designing learning experiences that build on student curiosity should be a priority in every classroom. The way we pose questions to students as teachers, with our language and framing choices, can spark curiosity. Simply introducing a small gap in knowledge can stimulate student curiosity: for example, "I wonder why these animals eat different foods?" or "I wonder why that algorithm didn't work?" This type of inquiry creates opportunities for students to engage, reflect, and explore, and supports a classroom culture that is consistently curious (Badley, 2012; Jirout et al., 2018). An additional way to promote classroom curiosity can be achieved when a teacher creates levels of uncertainty to stimulate curiosity (Jirout et al., 2018). Facilitating contexts and conditions for learning that drive students to discover is invigorating; placing value on student inquiry over correct answers produces space for students to accept a teacher's open-ended invitation to learning. Making the most of students' questions rather than ignoring their questions can also influence students' curious nature (Audet & Jordan, 2005).

At the end of my first year of teaching junior high English, one of my students wrote me a note that captured his genuine spirit of curiosity. Chris (a pseudonym) wrote: *Thank you for making the effort to help others notice the wonders of the written word. I truly appreciate your dedicating your working career to revealing great authors to kids. If it wasn't for teachers such as yourself, the world would bear a very grim, foreboding future.* Chris' note, which I have framed in my office, conveys curiosity with a bit of humor in all the best ways. His words serve to inspire me years after he was a student in my class. As I teach and learn alongside students like Chris, I strive to nurture my own spirit of curiosity. I hope you will join me. Together, we can build on and activate our own curiosity to create classrooms that possess and convey curiosity as the norm. Are you *curious* to see what might happen if we do?

Pause and Reflect

1. Consider and name three explicit ways you convey a spirit of curiosity for students. How do students respond when you demonstrate curiosity?
2. When you become innately curious, how do you feel inside?
3. How might you help your students distinguish between getting a quick answer from an internet resource and taking time to see knowledge through a lens of wonder or inquiry?
4. Which classroom conditions can you create so that student curiosity can flourish?
5. How might you pass on a spirit of curiosity to colleagues? Can you become an ambassador of curiosity?

References

Anderman, E. M., & Martinez Calvit, A. I. (2022). Is your deeper learning instruction boring students? *Educational Leadership, 79*(4), 33–37. http://www.ascd.org/

Audet, R., & Jordan, L. K. (Eds.). (2005). *Integrating inquiry across the curriculum.* Corwin Press.

Badley, K. (2012). Wonder. In A. L. Dee, & G. Tiffin (Eds.), *Faithful education: Themes and values for teaching, learning and leading.* Pickwick Publications.

Bain, K. (2004). *What the best college teachers do*. Harvard University Press.

Ballock, E. (2020). Zest, character education, and the common good. *International Christian Community of Teacher Educators Journal*, *15*(2). https://digitalcommons.georgefox.edu/icctej/vol15/iss2/4/

Brooks, D. (2023) The essential skills for being human. The New York Times. https://www.nytimes.com/2023/10/19/opinion/social-skills-connection.html?searchResultPosition=1

Day, C. (2004). *A passion for teaching*. RoutledgeFalmer.

Department of Education Dispositions Statement (2021). In Westmont Department of Education Teacher Credential Program Handbook 2022-2023, p. 5. https://www.westmont.edu/sites/default/files/users/user451/Teacher%20Credential%20Handbook%20for%20Printing_0.pdf

Dewey, J. (1906). *The child and the curriculum*. University of Chicago Press.

Dewey, J. (1938). *Experience and education*. Kappa Delta Pi.

Gallagher, J. (2023,). Let's bring joy back into learning. *Association for Supervision and Curriculum Development Blog*. https://www.ascd.org/blogs/lets-bring-joy-back-into-learning

Goodwin, B. (2022). Yes, you can motivate your students. *Educational Leadership*, *79*(4), 84–85. https://www.ascd.org/el/articles/research-matters-yes-you-can-motivate-your-students

Griffiths, P. (2009). *Intellectual appetite*. Catholic University of America Press.

Hargreaves, A. (2021). The future of learning lies in engagement. *Educational Leadership*, *79*(4), 26–31. https://www.ascd.org/el/articles/the-future-of-learning-lies-in-engagement

Jirout, J. J., Vitiello, V. E., & Zumbrunn, S. K. (2018). Curiosity in schools. *The New Science of Curiosity*, *1*(1), 243–266.

Joseph, D. C. (2022). The wisdom in questions. *International Christian Community of Teacher Educators Journal*, *17*(2). https://doi.org/10.55221/1932-7846.1284

Kidd, C., & Hayden, B. Y. (2015). The psychology and neuroscience of curiosity. *Neuron*, *88*(3), 449–460. https://doi.org/10.1016/j.neuron.2015.09.010

Malesic, J. (2023,). The key to success in college is so simple, it's almost never mentioned. New York Times Opinion. https://www.nytimes.com/2023/01/03/opinion/college-learning-students-success.html

Meadows, E. (2006). Preparing teachers to be curious, open minded, and actively reflective: Dewey's ideas reconsidered. *Action in Teacher Education*, *28*(2), 4–14. https://doi.org/10.1080/01626620.2006.10463406

Merriam Webster (2023). Curiosity. *In Merriam-Webster.com Dictionary*. https://www.merriam-webster.com/dictionary/curiosity

Pluck, G., & Johnson, H. L. (2011). Stimulating curiosity to enhance learning. *General Sciences and Psychology*, *2*(19), 24–31.

Wilson, J. T. (2010). Students' perspective on intrinsic motivation to learn: A model to guide educators. *International Christian Community of Teacher Educators Journal*, *6*(1). https://digitalcommons.georgefox.edu/cgi/viewcontent.cgi?article=1072&context=icctej

Yamada, K. (2013). *What do you do with an idea?* Compendium, Inc.

Zurn, P., & Bassett, D. (2018). On curiosity: A fundamental aspect of personality, a practice of network growth. *Personality Neuroscience*, *1*, E13. https://www.cambridge.org/core/journals/personality-neuroscience/article/on-curiosity-a-fundamental-aspect-of-personality-a-practice-of-network-growth/CFA46ADDF0000FA1CB3321EF7A7EA97A

3

Reflection

Reflection is Integral to Teaching

In *Joyful Resilience as Educational Practice* (Hughes & Badley, 2022), a book I co-edited with my colleague and friend, Ken Badley, we address the reciprocal nature of teaching and the unexpected rewards that teaching bestows on teachers. Individuals choose to teach in order to give back to society, to pay it forward, to inspire young minds. Most individuals do not choose teaching for a paycheck, or recognition, or because the profession is glamorous. We know that none of these reasons are true! A majority of teachers choose to teach because of the intrinsic nature of the profession: the "ah-ha!" moment when a student understands new content, poses an interesting question, demonstrates curiosity, or expresses awe for new knowledge. After *Joyful Resilience as Educational Practice* was published, I realized that every chapter in the book, whether written by my co-editor, myself, or another colleague, identified reflection as part of a teacher's DNA. Every teacher knows that reflection requires intentionality. It is rare to read anything on topics related to education or the teaching profession without finding a correlation to reflection. When educators reflect, we make a choice, a conscious decision, to grow and learn. Reflective professional practice enriches our lives and invigorates a commitment to our teacher selves, our calling to teach, and our beliefs (Antaya-Moore & Neal, 2022). If the disposition of reflection is integral

DOI: 10.4324/9781003379539-3

to our work, how do we nurture habits of reflection and make them stick?

Reflection elicits contemplation or consideration of an idea or a set of ideas. Reflection means giving serious thought to something, thinking quietly and calmly about some subject matter, idea or purpose (Merriam-Webster, 2023). We see reflection at work when a teacher makes small adjustments for the next class or when a teacher concludes teaching a large unit. We also see reflection when a teacher discusses assessment data or a struggling student with a colleague. For some educators, reflection comes naturally, but for others, reflection requires intentionality and action. In my pre-service program, my colleagues and I prioritize and explicitly name that becoming a *reflective practitioner* is essential to a teacher's training and experience. Student teachers, alongside faculty, are challenged to seek to develop and "display a willingness to think flexibly, adapt, and develop habits for growth and self-awareness" (Department of Education Dispositions Statement, 2021,p. 5). Student teachers are routinely asked to journal about their clinical experiences; reflect and write papers after they have planned and taught lessons; view and reflect on video recordings of their teaching; and analyze and develop sections of lessons that need to be strengthened. They are also asked to reflect in class among an audience of their peers as well as in K-12 classrooms with their cooperating teachers and students. In my experience, through time and practice, reflection becomes a way of doing, being, and a habit of mind that student teachers embrace and practice. Educator and author Shelly Sherman asserts that habits of reflection occur when pre-service candidates are prompted to develop dispositions in a variety of contexts; nurturing dispositions in practice in fieldwork and coursework contexts gives candidates opportunities to reflect and respond (2013). Curiously, I find that when a student teacher completes our pre-service program and is recommended for a credential, they are no longer required by program faculty to reflect regularly. As a result, when reflection is no longer expected in a new teacher's first teaching position, intentional space for reflection must be created. In a first teaching position, a new teacher's focus shifts from being required to reflect as a student, to making intentional efforts to reflect as a professional in order to create a sense of ownership. Creating reflective routine becomes critical. Reflection may take a different form from person to person or educator to educator, but the training and habitual practice ensures, in both small and big ways, that reflection is integrated into a teacher's daily work.

The Reality of Reflection

For many years, after a day of teaching, when my faculty colleague Laura (a pseudonym) and I would return to our offices, we would ask each other, "How did your class go?" or "How was your lesson today?" After a few weeks engaging in these exchanges, I enlisted a baseball metaphor: "I think I hit [my lesson] to second base today!" or "Today, [my lesson] was a home run!" These collegial exchanges led to deeper conversations about students and course content. Oftentimes, Laura and I would name and discuss lesson successes as well as trouble spots that were exposed in our lessons. As colleagues, we embraced and found comfort in the exchanges because they challenged our thinking as professionals. The act of reflecting together not only demonstrated our reflective practice efforts but also strengthened our habits of reflection that led to increased collaboration between us.

Researchers note that reflection requires an individual to take a personal experience, ponder it deeply, and learn from it (Hill-Jackson et al., 2019, p. 84). Reflection starts with and builds on the qualities a person possesses; when teachers consider who they want to become, their ambitions can be met (Korthagen et al., 2013). The COVID-19 pandemic created ample and unexpected opportunity for reflection. Moving to online instruction shifted the way teachers taught and the way students learned. Although educators thought about these topics pre-COVID, considering what was essential in the middle of a crisis forced us to revisit both who we are teaching and why we are teaching (DeHart, 2020). As a result, reflection has truly become an integral part of what we do as we consider, try, and implement solutions in times of crisis and even during traditional teaching days. Reflecting on what we do, our best practice, drives us to take action, make changes, and strengthen our work. I wholeheartedly believe that reflection is a non-negotiable disposition. For instance, if we want to learn to play the piano, we practice the same song over and over again; and when we want to learn how to make a three-point shot in basketball, we repeatedly shoot three-pointers on the court until we sink the shot. Similarly, teachers must engage in routine reflection to develop and internalize habits and skills of reflection.

A thoughtful colleague frames reflective practice as a means for educators to remain open to learning from students (Sullivan, 2022). She argues, from experience that recognizing her own failures as an educator has helped her look beyond thinking about her own teaching. Her reflective practice continues to evolve and reveals a greater openness to others that has sustained her as a professional. Staying engaged, as a reflective practitioner, grounds her in the ever-changing work. Similarly, another inspiring colleague writes about the dissonance, doubt, and disillusionment found in teaching. She pinpoints that teaching is a profoundly personal journey that impacts every part of the teacher self; in other words, reflecting on the dissonant moments in our field fuels a teacher to persevere rather than give up. When we befriend the benefits or the progress gained from the act of reflection, genuine learning and growth can ensue (Wall, 2022). Engaging in reflection and doing this work as humans and as teachers is essential because teaching requires continual self-reflection (Johnson, 2015). A 1992 study explored a teacher's thought life and a teacher's professional assumptions, personality, and repertoire (Palma & Millies, p. 28). The study affirmed the complexity of teaching and teacher experiences in and outside of the classroom while it also recognized reflection as a method for teachers to actively participate in their own professional growth.

Displaying a growth mindset or an attitude of "I haven't learned that *yet*" can also demonstrate a spirit of reflection. For growth to occur, an individual must possess an openness to reflect and develop professionally (Dweck, 2016). Most often shared with students, a growth mindset can also motivate teachers. For instance, if a student teacher's first literacy lesson flops in their clinical placement, as their supervisor, I will follow up the lesson with discussion about the reality that all teachers have lessons that flop. We will discuss why the lesson flopped, what was missing, and what can be strengthened. Acknowledging that student teachers aren't expected to master a literacy lesson or its delivery early in their pre-service program encourages student teachers to maintain a growth mindset in order to develop their craft. Framing a lesson flop with a statement such as, "I haven't learned that aspect of teaching literacy, *yet*," encourages growth. Just like mastering a song on the piano or sinking a three-point shot on the basketball court, reflection in practice fosters a desire to reflect more. I truly believe that reflection is the gift that keeps on giving. The more I reflect, the more I learn, and the more I want to reflect and learn!

Creating Habits of Reflection

American society generally associates success with multi-tasking, pushing the limits and accomplishing tasks quickly with a level of efficiency. Finding time to slow down feels counter-productive to the pace people seem to expect or keep as professionals. Ironically, research shows that people become more productive when they include rest into their routines (Miller, 2016; Smith, 2023). According to this research, rest can be exercise, sleep, or a simple ten-minute break. Rest can bring greater clarity and creativity when we incorporate its rhythms into our lives (Miller, 2016). Reflection can also cultivate creativity. I found this to be true during my sabbatical in 2017 after I read Shelly Miller's book, *Rhythms of Rest* (2016). The book invited me to reflect—to search for time and space for reflection and creativity. As a result, I found increased time to notice trees, flowers, and people on my neighborhood walks. I also found more time to think through my scholarship, which, as Miller describes and I learned, led to new ideas and professional creativity. Similarly, as mentioned in Chapter 2, the main character in Kobi Yamada's children's book, *What Do You Do with An Idea?* (2013), shares that he has an idea; yet, he wonders what to do with it. His inquiry grows not only his curiosity but his reflective nature when he realizes that the idea helps him see things differently, as well as makes space for creativity or potential change.

At the start of full-time student teaching each January, I ask my student teachers to consider how they will cultivate and demonstrate a reflective spirit in their classrooms. Responses typically range from writing a daily reflection to articulating highs and lows of the day, as well as naming and considering future goals and areas of growth. Later in the semester, when student teachers finish their full-time placements, I ask them to revisit their initial goals for reflection. When they do, student teachers typically see some of the idealism in their early goals juxtaposed with the reality of what they were able to accomplish in the semester. Reflecting over time, seeing and identifying professional challenges and growth, is always enlightening. I find that through reflective practice, student teachers often discover that they can identify and articulate growth that they hadn't seen before. Helping them develop a regular routine for reflection to identify progress as well as goals and growth truly strengthens their professionalism.

Additionally, as student teachers finish our program in the late spring, I encourage them to take a few weeks to disconnect, to catch their breath, and to not think about teaching. In due time, they return to reflection, naming and noticing all the things they learned, and all the areas they want to strengthen professionally. I find that student teachers miss, *yes, they miss*, the required reflection assignments from the pre-service program when they arrive in their first teaching positions. As a result, they must build on the intentional reflection routines and habits that work for them, whether it be through a written journal, an exchange over a meal with a colleague, or a more formal reflection with a school administrator. It's not surprising that reflection can pose an ongoing challenge for veteran teachers or those who may be disillusioned with the profession. Finding time to reflect individually or with colleagues, among all of the other classroom responsibilities, requires time, intentionality, and purpose; however, doing so honors a teacher's time as well as nurtures their growth and professionalism.

When humans aren't engaged or intellectually present, we aren't developing critical thinking skills; however, when we reflect, we become more engaged and present in tasks and our current reality. Engagement fosters the critical thinking skills that serve us in our personal and professional lives. Giving students mindfulness strategies to process thoughts, develop critical thinking, and build empathy becomes vital for students and teachers (Estrada, 2023). With thousands of thoughts running through our minds each day, reflection can lead teachers and students to greater self-awareness. Teachers can provide students reflective tools, as well as mindfulness techniques and space to practice them, which, in turn, creates space for students to think and reflect. Breathing, disconnecting, and engaging in mindfulness practices actually help individuals think more effectively. A mindfulness approach supports refreshment through rest, pause, and disconnection (Miller, 2016). When we take time to pause and rest, we generate space to reflect which can lead us to increased creativity and innovation.

Sixth-grade teacher Staci Korkowski recognizes that today's students don't need to only learn facts, but they also need time to reflect. They must develop critical thinking skills to think creatively and problem solve. During the last ten minutes of her class, several times a week, Korkowski decided to ask students to reflect and journal what they learned, whether they had met their learning goals, and what they still needed to help them achieve their learning goals. After several weeks of consistent reflective journaling, Kowkowski identified three themes: students expressed a positive outlook, showed increased confidence, and transferred their skills to daily life (2014). Efforts to teach and guide students through reflective journaling revealed deeper thinking that ultimately nurtured habits of reflection for both Kowkowski and her sixth graders. Reflective routines like these prepare students with skills for reflection well beyond the classroom.

Reflection for Growth

Accepting feedback from colleagues, mentors, administrators, or pre-service supervisors is another way to reflect and learn. Seeking feedback, whether through direct conversations, evaluations, or teaching observations, can be an asset. Considering what you can do better, identifying learning gaps, and noting what strategies to implement to try or improve are all methods to strengthen a teacher's reflective muscles. Hearkening back to my early days of teaching, I recall seeking help with a disruptive class. After weeks of trying new things with my junior high students, I felt overwhelmed and frustrated. In response, I mustered up some courage and decided to ask a school counselor for help. The counselor listened well as I shared about my classroom challenges, and then she offered to come observe my class the next day. Her observations were wise and succinct; she recommended that I move a few students' seats, find quiet ways to affirm students, and approach misbehaving students calmly. Most importantly, her feedback empowered me and I was able to regain my confidence as a teacher. I realized then, and still do today, that I am a work in progress. Through this early career experience, I learned how reflection could strengthen my teacher practice. Because I took the time to pause and reflect, I was able to ask for help and implement the feedback I received. Today, reflection continues to inform my decision-making as it did many years ago. Additionally, reflection yields wonderful rewards, and as teachers, we discover these rewards when our repeated reflective actions lead to habits and true growth.

A distinct and powerful facet of reflection is that it allows teachers to participate in their own growth. Reflection raises a teacher's consciousness about what they do, linking thought to action. As educators, by nature and with practice, we become more mindful of our professional skills and even our weaknesses when we reflect. Notably, teachers view themselves as professionals who have important choices to make, and their choices have a direct impact on their students (Koerner, 1992). Moreover, when teachers reflect, they become stronger and more effective teachers (Palma & Millies, 1992). As our perceptions change, our actions change; as we develop professionally, we build greater confidence that plays a profound role in our work. This type of awareness can be viewed as an intuitive skill that comes from an individual's lived and learned experiences, their knowledge, and their reflective efforts (Brooks, 2023). Dispositions truly strengthen our professionalism and reflection stands as significant to nourishing our teacher selves. Furthermore, consistent and routine reflection conveys deep care for the profession, for what we do for students, and for ourselves.

As you continue reading *Dispositions Are a Teacher's Greatest Strength*, I hope you will pause and reflect using the questions at the end of each chapter. Each disposition explored in this book is essential for productive, beneficial reflection. The 13 dispositions in this book, gratitude, courage, and collaboration to name a few, invite reflection; these dispositions inherently intertwine with reflection as a valuable thread that links the dispositions together. To teach, means we continue to learn (Koerner, p. 59). And reflection is a means for us to be open to learning and becoming. Reflecting with both heart and mind remains essential to a teacher's mindset and daily work (Day, 2004, p. 119). Will you accept the challenge to pause and reflect with me?

Pause and Reflect

1. When and where do you create space for professional reflection; how do you explicitly and implicitly reflect throughout a typical teaching day?

2. Consider "practicing" reflection with a colleague. Using the following questions, or perhaps the baseball analogy referenced at the beginning of this chapter, ask each other about your teaching? Name and discuss the "winning" parts of your lessons. What lesson aspects need to be strengthened?

3. When you carve out time for professional introspection what do you notice about your attitudes, thoughts, and actions?

4. Do you discover professional benefits when you routinely engage in reflection? Explain.

5. What contexts and conditions set the stage for you to be more innovative and creative?

References

Antaya-Moore, D., & Neal, J. (2022). Joyful defiance of constraints. In M. C. Hughes, & K. Badley (Eds.), *Joyful resilience as educational practice* (pp. 124–135). Taylor and Francis. https://doi.org/10.4324/9781003124429

Brooks, D. (2023). In the age of A. I., major in being human. The New York Times. https://www.nytimes.com/2023/02/02/opinion/ai-human-education.html

Day, C. (2004). *A passion for teaching*. RoutledgeFalmer.

DeHart, J. D. (2020). Sudden shift: Reflection on online learning. *Association of Middle Level Education Newsletter*. https://www.amle.org/sudden-shift-reflections-on-online-learning/

Department of Education Dispositions Statement (2021). In *Westmont Department of Education Teacher Credential Program Handbook 2022-2023*, p. 5. https://www.westmont.edu/sites/default/files/users/user451/Teacher%20Credential%20Handbook%20for%20Printing_0.pdf

Dweck, C. S. (2016). *Mindset: The new psychology of success* (updated edition). Ballentine Books.

Estrada, J. D. (2023). Going beyond thinking. *Educational Leadership*, *80*(7), 32–36. https://www.ascd.org/el/articles/going-beyond-thinking

Hill-Jackson, V., Hartlep, N. D., & Stafford, D. (2019). *What makes a star teacher: 7 dispositions that support student learning.*. ASCD.

Hughes, M. C., & Badley, K. (2022). *Joyful resilience as educational practice*. Taylor and Francis. https://doi.org/10.4324/9781003124429

Johnson, L. (2015). *Teaching outside the box: How to grab your students by their brains* (3rd ed.). Jossey-Bass.

Koerner, M. E. (1992). Teachers' images. In W. H. Schubert, & W. C. Ayers (Eds.), *Teacher lore: Learning from our own experience* (pp. 40–60). Longman Publishing Group.

Korkowski, S. (2014). Self-directed learning through reflection. *Association for Middle Level Education Magazine*. https://www.amle.org/self-directed-learning-through-reflection/

Korthagen, F. A. J., Kim, Y. M., & Greene, W. L. (2013). *Teaching and learning from within: A core reflection approach to quality and inspiration in education*. Routledge.

Merriam-Webster, (2023). Reflection. *In Merriam-Webster.com dictionary.* https://www.merriam-webster.com/dictionary/reflection

Miller, S. (2016). *Rhythms of rest.* Bethany House.

Palma, S., & Millies, G. (1992). The relationship between a teacher's life and teaching. In W. H. Schubert, & W. C. Ayers (Eds.), *Teacher lore: Learning from our own experience* (pp. 25–43). Longman Publishing Group.

Sherman, S. C. (2013). *Teacher preparation as an inspirational practice: Building capacities for responsiveness.* Routledge.

Smith, M. (2023). *The no. 1 habit that sets successful people apart from everyone else, says psychologist: It's a nonnegotiable.* CNBC Make it. https://www.cnbc.com/2023/03/12/psychologist-the-no-1-habit-that-sets-successfulhappy-people-apart.html

Sullivan, S. (2022). Sustainable teaching. In M.C. Hughes, & K. Badley (Eds.), *Joyful resilience as educational practice* (pp. 47–57). Taylor and Francis. https://doi.org/10.4324/9781003124429

Wall, C. R. G. (2022). Joyful resilience through dissonance, doubt, and disillusionment. In M. C. Hughes, & K. Badley (Eds.), *Joyful resilience as educational practice* (pp. 111–123). Taylor and Francis. https://doi.org/10.4324/9781003124429

Yamada, K. (2013). *What do you do with an idea?* Compendium.

4

Empathy

An Overview of Empathy

Every September, my college's Education Department hosts an annual gathering for K-12 educators. Local educators share encouraging stories at this gathering in an effort to convey that collectively we are not alone as we strive to serve, teach, and care for our students and colleagues. We recently chose the theme of empathy for the event because day in and day out, teachers often feel weary and overwhelmed with stacks of grading and exams to give, meetings to attend, parent conferences to prepare for, and student behaviors to manage. To put it simply, a teacher's email in box is full literally and figuratively. As one of my students would say, "I don't have any more data or bandwidth!" Or put another way, "I've reached maximum capacity!"

Teaching has always been complex and complicated work. It's emotionally challenging work. Post-pandemic, many teachers feel considerable loss and grief as they carry concerns for students, families, and colleagues. Despite the unique present-day circumstances, teachers continue to forge ahead without a clear roadmap. The last few years truly stretched educators' limits, taking Nel Noddings' ethic of care (2003) to new levels of nurturing and love. Teaching post-pandemic, I've realized that the new normal feels like a space where I have often given my all and done my best; yet, I'm often unsure that I've always *been at* my best. Serving students and colleagues in this uncharted

DOI: 10.4324/9781003379539-4

territory continues to tax educators intellectually, emotionally, personally, and professionally.

As we consider the disposition of empathy, it is important to distinguish the difference between compassion and empathy. Compassion is typically seen when a person conveys sympathy or concern, whereas demonstrated empathy looks to really understand another's feelings and perspective. These two dispositions have a considerable amount of overlap; however, for the deep and personal work we do with students and for the purpose of this chapter, I will focus on the disposition of empathy. And while empathy is integral to our work as teachers, it is important to acknowledge that empathy can be exhausting. Carrying students' burdens and engaging in emotional heavy lifting can be draining. As teachers cultivate empathy, we must be aware of over-extending ourselves as we address and hold students' burdens. Whether we answer late night emails or stay after school to review content with students, we must be mindful to set boundaries to guard our own emotional capacity.

Shared Empathy

As I contemplate the times when I offer empathy to a hurting student or receive empathy from another person, many memories come to mind. I recall a conversation with a student in which I was able to listen and even shed tears with the student over a painful misunderstanding she'd experienced. I also remember a time when another student came to me struggling with a decision about her future. The student needed acknowledgment that it was okay for her to sit in uncertainty and not make a hasty decision. I also recall a time when I witnessed one colleague say to another, "That must have been really difficult and painful." When I heard these words, they echoed deeply in my heart as I recognized my colleague making genuine efforts to empathize— to seek to understand and care deeply.

Sharing empathy means an individual has the ability to connect to others' emotions—anxiety, fear, or sadness. In their book, *Teach with Your Strengths*, authors Rosanne Liesveld and

Jo Ann Miller frame empathy as emotional intelligence or possessing "emotional radar" (2005, p. 113). Unlike sharing sympathy, a feeling of concern for another person's difficult situation, empathy involves "sharing in the emotional experience of the other person" (Merriam-Webster, 2023). Empathy includes acknowledging and seeking to understand another individual's feelings of pain, angst, worry, or distress. Dispositions like empathy serve our moral compass, helping to guide our understanding, self-awareness, and behaviors. Author Elena Aguilar defines empathy as feeling another individual's pain (2018, p. 121). She skillfully uses the image of a spider web to explain that when we share moments of empathy with others, the moments become significant connections and like a web, they hold us together through challenges that make us feel seen and heard. These instances build our resilience as well as build our capacity for empathy. Additionally, empathetic responses build trust, strengthen relationships, and can even expand an individual's worldview; yet, teachers, according to Aguilar, can carry tensions that may hold both hope and pain for students. Inasmuch as we feel another's pain, empathy can feel complicated; it can be challenging to empathize with those that are unlike us or those that we feel are harder to connect with (Spencer, 2010, p. 177). Even so, when our capacity to understand students grows, opportunities to reach students also grows (Whitaker, 2012). The more we can express our own emotions, the better we can become at identifying emotions in others (Luckner & Rudolph, 2010). "As educators, we display compassion and empathy through our nuanced knowledge of students—their capacities and possibilities as well as their difficulties, anxieties, and vulnerabilities" (Wineberg, 2012, p. 43). Such demonstrations of care result in seeing our students well (Anderson, 2020).

While demonstrating empathy can take many forms, a central aspect of empathy is understanding and responding from another's point of view as if it was your own. This does not mean that you agree with the other person's perspectives or decisions, but your empathetic responses communicate "I am here," or "I see you," or "I am listening." To understand this aspect of empathy more deeply, several years ago, I knocked on several colleagues' office doors and asked them to demonstrate a variety of facial expressions that convey empathy. Faculty colleagues tilted their heads, some squinted a bit, others leaned in, some frowned, and many softened their expressions. I took photographs of the expressions and later shared them with my student teachers to prompt discussion about how to convey empathy to K-12 students. My students quickly noticed how the empathetic expressions seemed to communicate an understanding of another's angst, heartache, or sorrow. Together, my students and I realized that empathy can be felt and it can also be seen. Likewise, when students observe or feel sincere emotion coming from a teacher, they see the teacher as human which can be motivating for students; students learn more from teachers who engage emotionally with them (Liesveld & Miller, 2005).

Educator and author Kyle Schwartz inspires me to see, engage with, and understand my students more deeply. Schwartz' book, *I Wish My Teacher Knew* (2016), sprung out of a classroom activity that she shared on social media. Schwartz sought to actively foster relationships and community in her third-grade classroom by asking her students to respond to the prompt, "I wish my teacher knew." In response, her students shared specifics about what she didn't know about their home lives, school supply needs, and strengths. Students' heartfelt responses about their parents' busy work schedules or their lack of internet service at home highlighted ways Schwartz could practice empathy and act on it. In recent years, I have implemented Schwartz' "I wish my teacher knew" activity with my own undergraduates and each time, I find that my students are moved to not only try the activity with their own K-12 students but they also convey an increased desire to connect, empathize with, and truly seek to understand their students' diverse experiences. It is important to point out that while empathy is often conveyed verbally and physically, the disposition can be demonstrated in non-verbal ways such as when a teacher makes an internal decision to ignore a behavior or disruption. As teachers, we seek to know our students, we take pride in developing relationships with them, and we want to identify what motivates them and makes them tick. At the same time, teachers know when a student has reached their limit of focus, when they need a time-out, a recess break, or a moment to put their head on their desk to rest. Recognizing these instances as opportunities to quietly convey empathy can be just as powerful a tool as verbally acknowledging a student's pain or distress. Educator Louanne Johnson suggests that for teachers to develop increased skills of empathy, they shouldn't be afraid to be uncomfortable. For instance, she recommends that teachers enroll in a class in a content area where they don't feel confident or that they try a new hobby or sport, because when teachers embrace the uncomfortable, they not only develop greater empathy but they create space to feel some of the struggle and discomfort that students feel (Johnson, 2015, p. 241).

Early on in our pre-service program, when student teachers consider how they will cultivate and demonstrate empathy in their classrooms, we discuss how listening well will help them learn about students and better understand who they are. Later in the program, when student teachers complete their full-time clinical placements, I ask them to revisit their initial thoughts and goals for demonstrating empathy. Helping them see the reality of what it takes to convey empathy usually surprises student teachers. For instance, they find that because they have been present and accessible to their own students, they really value their students. They actually see their students as more than students; their students are humans *and* learners with interests and passions. Additionally, student teachers realize that when they make themselves accessible to their own students, in turn, their students trust them with their stories and needs. These empathetic actions and attitudes influence and enrich student teachers' relationships with students. Simple acts of listening to understand or sensing another person's emotions can uncover K-12 students' hurts and worries as well as encourage a student teacher to consider how to best respond to their students' feelings.

As I ponder empathy, I am reminded of an experience early in my career that I referred to in Chapter 1: a principal told me to never let my students see me cry. I followed the instructions initially, but in the years since, I have actually shed tears with students. Understanding that much of the work of teaching is emotionally heavy work that feels hard and taxing, I now believe that tears in certain instances are powerful and appropriate empathetic tools. In the rare circumstance, for example, where my faculty team faces making decisions about whether a student teacher should continue in our program or not, I am grateful to have a team that prioritizes empathy in our work. Protecting relationships with students and listening to students to understand are priorities for our team—even when it feels uncomfortable. Thinking through challenging decisions also requires thinking through the impact of the decisions on our students. Over time, I have discovered that practicing empathy requires intentionality and care *and* even a few tears. In full transparency, I haven't always handled difficult conversations with students, or colleagues, with great empathy, but I have realized that intentional and active listening has increased the depth of care I am able to communicate and my empathetic responses have evolved over time. I don't share this anecdote to toot my own horn, nor do I want to give readers the impression that I am hardened to difficult decisions that affect my students deeply. Instead, I hope to shine a light on empathy, a disposition and strength of the heart that requires practice and care.

In Charlie Mackesy's beautiful book, *The Boy, the Mole, the Fox and the Horse* (2019), the main character, the boy, asks, "What do we do when our hearts hurt?" His friend, the horse, responds, "We wrap them with friendship, share tears and time, till they wake hopeful and happy again" (p. 111). This response captures the essence of empathy with reference to an experience between friends with shared tears. Similarly, artist and writer Morgan Harper Nichols suggests that empathy is seen when we extend an open door to others and consider how it feels to walk in their shoes (2018). Educators hold their hearts open and numerous doors open for students; they wrap them in care, share their tears, and empathize with them regularly. These notable responses don't just happen; they must be nurtured thoughtfully.

Author and educator Jessica Cabeen suggests leading with empathy by recognizing and being yourself first rather than your title—for instance, I'm Michelle first and a teacher second. Cabeen recommends listening, learning, and caring as a powerful way to invest in others. Really striving to get to know others well—whether colleagues, parents, or students—demonstrates empathy in thoughtful ways. Educators can lead with purpose when they demonstrate vulnerability and honest authenticity in conversations so to learn from others. Cabeen claims, "Educators are the bravest people I know. You get up, show up, and demonstrate such character in the face of adversity from all angles" (Cabeen, 2019, p. 90). What's more, when individuals demonstrate empathy, they not only give to others but they in turn give to themselves.

Affective dispositions like empathy contribute positively to student and academic success (Huitt, 2005). Dispositions link to all the things that we teach, plan, execute, and assess. Student learning and achievement are most often the end goal, but we must first be human and consider the humanity of our students (DeHart, 2020). Connecting with others so we know we are not alone when we are challenged or struggling personifies empathy. Students, the humans we teach, not the assignment deadlines or the lesson plans, must remain our focus. As difficult as it can be to shift the focus from one's self to others, it's beneficial to feel and convey empathy for those around us who may be experiencing instability, anxiety, or other unseen difficulties. Empathetic perspective taking is a skill we can model and teach to help our students see others' points of view. What's more, when we prepare teachers and students with social and emotional competencies, they understand themselves and others better (Weissberg, 2021); thus, empowering students (and teachers) with the disposition of empathy will benefit others well beyond our classroom walls.

Empathy for Impact

Developing a teacher's empathy can elevate our work and connection with students. In 2022, The Association of Middle Level Education (AMLE), gathered a group of teacher leaders and school administrators to discuss and define empathy in their work. The group discovered a link between empathy and attentive, active listening; to actively listen means putting yourself in another's shoes to validate their experiences and perspective. The group noted that listening well often requires hearing concerns without passing judgment; it requires being present and honoring diverse perspectives. Hence, vulnerability and learning from one another leads to growth for everyone involved—including students (Engle et al., 2022). Demonstrating empathy, standing in a student's shoes, happens in different contexts. For instance, empathy can translate into practical and simple acts such as sitting with a student when they are upset or acknowledging a student's return to school after an illness. Recognizing a student's grief after they experience the loss of a family pet or acknowledging a student's frustration over a forgotten homework assignment are additional ways to empathize with students. Looking deeper, below the surface, and past a student's behavior or appearance can foster teacher empathy in practice (Wormeli, 2014).

In addition, routine check-ins with students—both academic and emotional check-ins—can also quietly communicate empathy and care for students. Teachers regularly ask students, "Are you ready to learn?" This type of question helps us understand our students and assess how they are feeling so we can then use their responses to inform and adjust our instruction (Wormeli, 2014). Consistent check-ins with students are a practical way to assess the figurative temperature or pulse of our students. Asking students for a thumbs up or thumbs down, inviting them to share a favorite emoji to demonstrate how they feel, or surveying students' emotions on a 1–5 point scale with a show of hands are practical approaches that gauge students' academic attitudes and emotions for learning. One high school teacher I know routinely gives students the opportunity to share about their lives at the beginning of class. Students typically share about their weekends, their sports' teams' scores, and their homework stressors. This same teacher also carefully reads through students' daily journal entries to assess students' mindsets for learning. Another junior high school teacher I know prioritizes looking students in the eyes to listen attentively when they want to share something. These intentional actions acknowledge that whatever is important to a student is also valued by the teacher.

In the same way that teachers support students with empathy, principals can also support teachers with empathy. Author and educator Jen Schwanke suggests that when school leaders look at motivators that highlight teachers' patterns, priorities, and purpose when things are going well and when they are not, they develop increased empathy for teachers (2022, p. 13). When teachers are known and seen by their school's leadership team, they feel supported. Similarly, schools and districts can consider reaching out to parents to increase their empathetic lenses. During the pandemic, for example, one school district initiated a listening practice with parents called empathy interviews. Through a series of carefully crafted open-ended interview questions, school liaisons posed questions to parents about their personal learning experiences, school memories, and hopes for school change. The interview data was used to inform district decisions and priorities, while at the same time, strengthened trust and community relationships. Whether educators take the time to know and understand students, teachers, or parents, they honor the others' voices, opinions, and stories and the efforts convey empathy in distinct and thoughtful ways.

I find that when I take the time to empathize with others, my guard comes down, my posture softens, and I lean in to listen to understand. Mark, a high school student who was often getting "into trouble" with his teachers, taught me a lot about empathy. Because Mark was a regular visitor to my assistant principal office, I often felt frustrated that I couldn't seem to form a connection with him. As a result, when I saw him heading to my office, I would think to myself, "Oh no, he's back!" Thankfully, a colleague on campus graciously took Mark under her wing and learned that he lived with his grandparents and cousins in a small one-bedroom apartment. Mark actually slept under the dining room table at night because he didn't have his own bed or bedroom. Once I learned these details about his circumstances, my attitude softened and my empathetic lens grew. My learned response toward Mark quickly changed and whenever I saw him coming my way, I greeted him with a smile, asked him questions, and leaned in to listen. Seeing Mark and his circumstances differently allowed me to understand him and gratefully our connection grew.

As you've seen so far in *Dispositions Are a Teacher's Greatest Strength*, exhibiting dispositions can take a variety of forms. And conveying the disposition of empathy can truly elevate our work and professionalism. Validating and understanding students' interests, concerns, and feelings are practical ways we can communicate empathy to students. Looking to see our students' hearts and who our students really are, beyond their appearance and behaviors, remains a vital aspect of teacher practice. Additionally, learning about ourselves, whether we are a teacher or a student increases our self-awareness. Author and psychologist Brené Brown thoughtfully affirms that empathy is about human connection (2018). Actively listening, helping a student or colleague know they are not alone, elevates our human connection. I often ask my student teachers to visualize what is in a student's physical and figurative backpack (Hughes, 2014). While the physical backpack may hold a lunchbox or notebook, there may also be hidden pain, anxiety, or burdens that students bring to school with them that we don't see. Seeking to know and understand what's in another's backpack helps educators, like you and me, expand our empathetic lenses and hearts for others. Shall we make concerted efforts to develop empathy, to look for opportunities to see each other, understand each other, and develop connections to expand our own hearts and appreciate the hearts of others?

Pause and Reflect

1. How might you elevate your listening skills even when it feels uncomfortable?
2. Reflect on an instance when you "stood in a student's shoes?" What did you discover about the student and yourself?
3. Consider a professional experience or instance when you felt both empathy and vulnerability? How might the experience inform your future interactions with students?
4. Reflect on an experience when you felt challenged to develop your empathetic skills for a colleague. Were you able to authentically convey empathy and shift your perspective? Why or why not?
5. What is one strategy you can implement to increase your sense of empathy for school leaders in your school community?

References

Aguilar, E. (2018). *Onward: Cultivating emotional resilience in educators.* Jossey Bass.

Anderson, D. W. (2020). The ethic of care and inclusive education. In Shotsberger, P., & Freytag, C. (Eds.), *How shall we then care?* Wipf and Stock.

Brown, B. (2018). *Dare to lead.* Random House.

Cabeen, J. (2019). *Lead with grace.* Times 10 Publications.

DeHart, J. D. (2020). *Sudden shift: Reflection on online learning.* Association for Middle Level Education Newsletter.https://www.amle.org/sudden-shift-reflections-on-online-learning/

Engle, K., Rigg, L., & Vosk, M. (2022). *Part one – six: Fostering empathy through understanding.* Association for Middle Level Education Newsletter.https://www.amle.org/fostering-empathy-through-understanding-listening-to-the-voices-of-administrators-and-teacher-leaders/

Hughes, M. C. (2014). What's in your backpack? *Association for Middle Level Education Magazine, 1*(9), 19.

Huitt, W. (2005). Important affective dispositions: Optimism, enthusiasm, and empathy. *Educational psychology interactive.* Valdosta State University. http://www.edpsycinteractive.org/topics/affect/optenth.html

Johnson, L. (2015). *Teaching outside the box: How to grab your students by their brains* (3rd ed.). Jossey-Bass.

Liesveld, R., & Miller, J. A. (2005). *Teach with your strengths: How great teachers inspire their students.* Gallup Press.

Luckner, J., & Rudolph, S. (2010). *Teach well, live well: Strategies for success.* Corwin.

Mackesy, C. (2019). *The boy, the mole, the fox and the horse.* Harper One.

Merriam-Webster. (2023). Empathy. In Merriam-Webster.com Dictionary. https://www.merriam-webster.com/dictionary/empathy

Nichols, M. H. (2018) [@morganharpernichols]. Empathy let me hold the door for you. Instagram. https://www.instagram.com/morganharpernichols/?hl=en

Noddings, N. (2003). *Caring: A feminine approach to ethics and moral education* (2nd ed.). University of California Press.

Schwanke, J. (2022). Motivational pull. *Educational Leadership, 80*(2), 12–13. https://www.ascd.org/el/articles/motivational-pull

Schwartz, K. (2016). *I wish my teacher knew: How one question can change everything for kids*. De Capo Lifelong Books.

Spencer, G. (2010). *Awakening the quieter virtues*. IVP Books.

Weissberg, R. P. (2021). The healing power of social and emotional learning. *The Sunday Paper.* https://mariashriver.com/the-healing-power-of-social-and-emotional-learning/

Whitaker, T. (2012). *What great teachers do differently: 17 things that matter most* (2nd ed.). Eye on Education.

Wineberg, T. (2012). Metaphors for teaching. In K. Badley, & H. Van Brummelen (Eds.), *Metaphors we teach by: How metaphors shape what we do in classrooms* (pp. 32–51). Wipf and Stock.

Wormeli, R. (2014). Building empathy. *Association for Middle Level Education Magazine.* https://www.amle.org/building-empathy/

5

Adaptability

Teachers as Chameleons

Historically, educators must make adjustments and adapt. Whether there is a new district or school policy, or a fresh technology platform, or a polished set of state or national standards, educators must be ready to adapt. Adaptability requires flexibility to shift and adjust to new conditions and situations (Merriam-Webster, 2023); teachers apply and internalize adaptability over time. Identifying when teachers demonstrate professional adaptability merits my attention as a pre-service faculty member. Nurturing a student teacher's self-awareness and ability to adapt are significant end goals that I work toward. When I present the disposition of adaptability in the introductory education class I teach, I share a visual image of a colorful chameleon. I next pose the question, "What does a teacher have in common with a chameleon?" One by one, students share that a chameleon is colorful and reminds them of the creativity a teacher must possess. Students often extend this thinking, remarking that reptiles have the unique ability to adjust to their circumstances and change their body color. I appreciate the chameleon analogy because it helps students visualize how teachers must be attentive and ready to change their attitudes and behaviors as well as their instructional and pedagogical approaches as they move between activities. Teachers make countless daily decisions and consider

DOI: 10.4324/9781003379539-5

logistics, classroom management, student behavior, and instruction; whether thinking about pacing, length of instructional activities, options for art projects, or timing for extended discussions, a teacher can cultivate skills of adaptability with time and practice.

By nature, teaching can feel unpredictable; therefore, it is important to acknowledge that the unpredictability can feel hard and actually be challenging. Educators are aware that there are never-ending shifts and adjustments to be made in their classrooms, schools, and districts. Whether they experience a major crisis in their school community or a small scheduling hiccup during their teaching day, they show up, adapt, and respond. It is part of the job. Practicing and developing skills for adaptability, being open to adapt, influences our mindset and behavior (Derler & Ray, 2019). Brain research reveals that our brains actually respond differently depending on our perceptions; when we perceive change as a threat, we feel distress; however, when we view change as an opportunity, we respond more positively and feel less distress (Derler & Ray, 2019; Jensen, 2008). Developing skills and mindsets to adapt can help us shift professionally and thrive in our daily work.

Research shows that, "Adaptability is an important capacity for thriving and effective teachers" (Granziera et al., 2019, p. 60); adaptability includes a breadth of emotional, behavioral, and cognitive considerations that are linked to positive student and teacher outcomes. Notably, a study of secondary school teachers suggests that when teachers are adaptable, they have increased well-being and their students have higher achievement rates (Collie et al., 2018). According to this study, adaptability denotes navigating uncertainty and change effectively—pondering options, adjusting thinking, and adapting emotions. When teachers are more adaptable, they are more committed to their jobs; when teachers feel they have more support from their school's leaders, they also demonstrate greater adaptability. The study concludes that adaptability supports teacher well-being and may even promote teacher retention; therefore, as we prepare new teachers and strive to retain experienced teachers, we must invest in the disposition of adaptability in hopes of empowering teachers to tackle education's ever-changing demands. Role play, mini-lessons, scenario-based learning, and engagement with practitioners are strategic methods that can help prepare new teachers who will eventually have classrooms of their own.

Affirming the benefits of adaptability, educator Dru Tomlin suggests that when educators are flexible, change can happen. Tomlin understands the demand for flexibility in teacher practice firsthand with lesson planning and homework design, while at the same time, she notes that adaptability is essential for students' goal-setting and achievement. In addition, she claims that being able to bend and adapt helps students navigate change and uncertainty (2021), much like the disposition of resilience explored in Chapter 6. In his latest book, *The Art of Teaching Children*, author Philip Done captures the pressure some teachers feel setting up "pinterest perfect" classrooms with fancy bulletin boards and desk décor; his humorous reference to the perfect classroom reminds me that teachers must be ready to adapt as soon as students enter their classrooms (2022, pp. 78–79). Classrooms are filled with imperfect students, imperfect teachers, unique situations, and sometimes unanticipated chaos that require great adjustment and flexibility. Ensuring that students feel cared for far outweighs the "picture perfect" classroom and affirms adaptability as a critical life skill that can empower teachers and students inside and outside the classroom.

The Time is Now

The educational challenges found in the present moment have opened doors for educators to be open-minded and reflective re-thinkers (Lewis, 2023, p. 41). Many school leaders recognize that today's educational landscape is suitable for creating change in schools and school systems (Reeves & Eaker, 2023). Even though the pandemic disrupted education as we know it, new routines, increased transparency, and online learning expanded (Hess, 2023). The present moment continues to create space for educational leaders to think outside the box and problem solve for school improvement.

Although school systems are sometimes characterized as organizations that resist change, they are typically eager to strengthen practice (Lewis, 2023). Collaborative efforts for continuous improvement remain a significant and ongoing end goal for most K-12 schools and districts. Although there are many established practices and strong systems, there are also realms that need refining or redefining. School leaders must be ready to adapt and shift their mindsets to embrace school or systematic change as a routine practice (New Leaders, 2023). Richard Culatta, the chief executive officer at the International Society for Technology in Education, recommends that when educators look to the future, they should distinguish between educational practices that are comfortable and practices that are effective (Rebora, 2023). Post-pandemic, Culatta affirms that new educational approaches require critical and relevant skills of adaptability. Arguing in favor of change-making—especially when the status quo isn't working or providing what is best for students—Culatta recognizes the importance of exploring and implementing innovative educational programs to move education forward.

Just as the disposition of adaptability is important for teachers to flourish, it is essential for school leaders to flourish. School leaders who embrace an adaptive leadership style typically have a clear vision and desire for constructive change and school improvement. They view problem solving, listening to diverse voices, and innovation as necessary components for change, coupled with mindsets that see adaptability as an opportunity for growth. According to author and educator, Jen Schwanke, taking a two-pronged approach to decision-making within a school community, using both the intellect and heart as essential tools, recognizes educators and school systems for who and what they are while at the same time ensures that protocols and policies are equitable, practical, and realistic (2023).

Go with the Flow

By nature, educators are creative people who like planning and innovation; teachers give oodles of time and attention to planning, creating, and differentiating lessons. Ironically, well thought-out plans don't always go according to plan. Whether there is a school electrical outage, safety drill, early dismissal, or rainy-day schedule, teachers are constantly assessing their next moves and making real-time decisions each time they set foot on their school campus. Teachers need to be ready to shift a lesson plan, adjust an expectation, or address a student's behavioral response. Alyson Klein, assistant editor for *Education Week*, reports that teachers make a bewildering 1,500 decisions a day (2021). This averages out to approximately three decisions per minute. Klein recognizes that teacher decision-making doesn't stop throughout a teacher's work day. From thinking through lessons plans, to navigating student absences and makeup work, to noticing and mitigating their own assumptions and biases in the classroom, teachers can end up feeling mentally and physically exhausted. Acknowledging the weight of decision-making that teachers feel, Klein became curious about how educators deal with the endless decision-making tasks. After asking several educators about their own decision-making, she offers a few strategies to tackle the plethora of tasks. She first suggests placing the role of decision-making in students' hands in order to allow them to have increased student ownership; she also recommends putting in the extra effort to make learning engaging.

Experienced teachers don't typically stop to think about or even realize the number of adjustments and decisions they make each day. Decision-making actually becomes natural, almost innate, through practice and increased experience in the classroom. Teachers may face gaining or losing a principal; a student may be moved to another teacher's classroom; or a student may be pulled out of class for an assessment. Because of unforeseen instances like these, educators must remain flexible so they can shift with the changing conditions.

One of my favorite parts of teaching is actually the creative aspect—thinking about how to frame thought-provoking questions, introduce new content, or adapt curriculum. Specifically, when I talk to student teachers about lesson planning or introducing new curriculum, I share about the value and power of hooking students into learning with new material. Whether a student teacher asks a larger essential question, shares an engaging visual image, or dangles a carrot of new knowledge to stimulate students' thinking, these interactions can feel invigorating. Brainstorming how to hook students into learning and guide them to a point of interest and curiosity fills my professional cup. Whether a teacher reteaches a section of a lesson plan or accommodates a student who has been absent for a number of weeks, teachers adapt. Phrases like "go with the flow," "just roll with it," or "roll with the punches" capture the reality of on-the-job decision-making as well as a teacher's willingness to adapt in order to serve students well.

Hoping to develop the disposition of adaptability in student teachers, I've realized that one of the most interesting aspects of the new-to-teaching experience is that student teachers are typically unable to hide what they are thinking. Early in a clinical placement, student teachers know that they will be confronted with a variety of instructional and management decisions in the classroom. Even so, they typically aren't yet comfortable in their own skin with in-the-moment decision-making because they haven't yet practiced it. When this happens, I often see student teachers pause to look for guidance from their cooperating teacher because they don't yet trust themselves or their ability to make on-the-spot decisions. During debriefing meetings, post-observations, I often share that I visualize speech balloons, like those in cartoon comics, above my student teachers' heads. The speech balloons represent a student teacher's internal thinking about responsibilities such as classroom management or possible responses to students' behavior or engagement. After a few weeks in the classroom, I usually notice that student teachers' imaginary speech balloons begin to fade away one by one. With time and practice, they begin to internalize their next moves and become able to adapt and make quick decisions. With increased experience, student teachers subconsciously move through each day adapting to students' needs and unexpected events feeling more confident. On-the-spot decision-making does not come easily to all student teachers (or all experienced teachers); some student teachers need more time or additional encouragement to develop this skill more than others. Nevertheless, if they are able to recognize what they need to do and are open to learning and trying, student teachers typically gain skills of adaptability and increased confidence.

I recently read about an inspiring teacher who displayed great adaptability when she examined and shifted her stance on homework (Torres, 2021); Christina Torres asked herself about each homework assignment she gave, the objectives and skills expected in the homework, and how each assignment served students. Wrestling with concerns about homework tools and access related to internet connections, computers, and school supplies, Torres chose to shift how she approached homework. As a result, she intentionally checked in with students individually, considered their learning styles alongside homework design, and pondered how the homework might benefit each student. This example highlights the power of one teacher's ability to adapt and reminds me of an experience I had with a student teacher named Sarah (a pseudonym). Sarah, who was consistently inquisitive, stayed after class one day and asked about the purpose of my course's summative assignment. Although I had already explained to the class of student teachers that the assignment was a demonstration of their work and progress throughout the preservice program, Sarah asked for additional clarification and support. I explained my rationale behind the assignment and after doing so, Sarah felt she could move forward and wholeheartedly invest in the assignment. This experience with Sarah reminded me of the importance of explicitly sharing the purpose behind each of my assignments. While some students require minimal context or explanation to get started on an assignment, others, like Sarah, need more details and support to understand and meet the targeted skills they will gain by doing the work. I am grateful for the interaction with Sarah because, unknowingly, Sarah nudged me to take more time to understand her needs, and consider all of my students' needs, as well as anticipate potential student misunderstandings (all of the things I attempt to teach my students). Sarah reminded me of the importance of remaining open and ready to adapt. Her thoughtful request was humbling and it also challenged me to do and be better.

Adaptability Generates Greater Adaptability

As I reflect on my skills of and for adaptability, I realize that I have demonstrated the disposition uniquely through each career season and circumstance. Early in my career, for example, my skills of adaptability developed as I learned to use my professional voice and respond to unexpected classroom interruptions. After a few years of teaching, I demonstrated additional skills of adaptability as I set goals for growth when I chose to refine my teaching with research, conferences, and additional education to earn a master's degree. I next became a high school administrator and quickly realized that I needed to give away the control I felt in my own classroom in exchange for a lack of schedule and uncertainty in my new role. Years later, when I entered higher education, I adapted once again to new teaching and tenure expectations in unfamiliar contexts. Each of these career seasons required me to shift and adjust. Every vocational milestone required me to adapt in new ways. Whether I was teaching a seventh grader or an undergraduate, offering my perspective in a committee meeting, or observing a student teacher, my readiness to adapt matured my skills and professional confidence. And like so many of the dispositions explored in *Dispositions Are a Teacher's Greatest Strength*, my ability to adapt has evolved as my career contexts have changed. My own experiences reinforce that teacher decisions, whether they are made innately without thinking or intentionally and consciously, help shape our habits and teacher character for the long-term (Dow, 2013, p. 144).

As we near the end of this chapter, can you recall a teaching day when all aspects of the day flowed seamlessly? Teachers like you and me experience and orchestrate days where there are smooth transitions between activities, minimal behavioral distractions, and students are skillfully led into learning. These types of days feel magical—and they help teachers remember our purpose, sense of calling, and love for teaching. At the same time, days like these still require adaptability. Smooth days and smooth lessons feel this way because a teacher has both pro-actively planned and actively adapted to the day's needs, both expected and spontaneous. Magical days don't occur without care, effort, practice, and profound flexibility. I find that the teaching days where I made the decision to "wing it" due to a full schedule or a poor night's sleep typically backfire. In con-trast, the days where I take the time to think about the students in my class, anticipate their needs, and consider any potential academic misunderstandings, pay off. The concerted effort produces reward for both my students and me. Nonetheless, planning well must work together *with* flexibility in order for a teacher's day to flow smoothly. Both are needed, because planning without flexibility can lead to frustration, but planning *with* flexibility can lead to anticipating the unexpected in order to pivot with grace.

Through the years, I have genuinely relished the times students left my class with a smile or an expression of gratitude, saying, "That was such a fun class!" or "I love the book we are reading!" Moments such as these feel like a gift, an affirmation of all the time and effort it takes to show up with an open heart ready to teach with flexibility and grace. Although the day-in and day-out practice of adaptability manifests in different ways with class interruptions, students' tangential questions, pencils thrown, or fire drills, each instance of adaptability actually strengthens a teacher's self-awareness and elevates every other aspect of their work. Just as Parker Palmer urges readers in *Let Your Life Speak* to honor the tensions and limits of our work without sacrificing our potential (2000, p. 55), teachers must harness skills of and for adaptability. Acknowledging the disposition of adaptability as a critical strength as we bend and grow reveals its hidden reward.

Pause and Reflect

1. Think back on the first days of your teaching career. How has the disposition of adaptability matured you professionally?
2. To what degree do you view adaptability as essential to classroom and career longevity and flourishing? Why or why not?
3. When have you made an in-the-moment decision that benefitted your students? What was the outcome and how did students respond?
4. What professional conditions and contexts provide space for you to develop increased adaptability?
5. What circumstances or barriers make adapting challenging for you in the workplace? How can you confront these circumstances with an open mind and heart?

References

Collie, R. J., Martin, A., & Granziera, H. (2018) *Being able to adapt in the classroom improves teachers' well-being.* UNSW Sydney Newsroom. https://newsroom.unsw.edu.au/news/social-affairs/being-able-adapt-classroom-improves-teachers-well-being

Derler, A., & Ray, J. (2019). *Why change is so hard—and how to deal with it.* Neuroleadership.com https://neuroleadership.com/your-brain-at-work/growth-mindset-deal-with-change

Done, P. (2022). *The art of teaching children.* Avid Reader Press.

Dow, P. E. (2013). *Virtuous minds: Intellectual character development.* IVP Academic.

Granziera, H., Collie, R. J., & Martin, A. J. (2019). Adaptability: An important capacity to cultivate among pre-service teachers in teacher education programmes. *Psychology Teaching Review, 25*(1), 60–66. https://eric.ed.gov/?id=EJ1216443

Hess, F. M. (2023). Moving from 'reform' to 'rethinking'. *Educational Leadership, 80*(6), 40–44.

Jensen, E. (2008). *Brain-based learning: The new paradigm of teaching* (2nd ed.). Corwin Press.

Klein, A. (2021). *1,500 decisions a day (at least!): How teachers cope with a dizzying array of questions.*https://www.edweek.org/teaching-learning/1-500-decisions-a-day-at-least-how-teachers-cope-with-a-dizzying array-of-questions/2021/12

Lewis, A. (2023). Getting to institutional-level change. *Educational Leadership, 80*(6), 26–31. https://www.ascd.org/el/articles/moving-from-reform-to-rethinking

Merriam-Webster (2023). Adaptability. In *Merriam-Webster Dictionary.* https://www.merriam-webster.com/dictionary/adaptability

New Leaders (2023). Adaptive leadership: How great school principals lead for change. https://www.newleaders.org/about/story

Palmer, P. J. (2000). *Let your life speak: Listening for the voice of vocation.* John Wiley & Sons.

Rebora, A. (2023). Richard Culatta on the "transitional moment" in education. *Educational Leadership, 80*(6), 14–19. https:www.ascd.org/el/articles/richard-culatta-on-the-transitional-moment-in-education

Reeves, D., & Eaker, R. (2023). Getting more urgent about change leadership. *Educational Leadership, 80*(6), 20–24. https://www.ascd.org/el/articles/getting-more-urgent-about-change-leadership

Schwanke, J. (2023). Heart and head: A principal's essential tools. *Educational Leadership, 81*(2). https://www.ascd.org/el/articles/heart-and-head-a-principals-essential-tools

Tomlin, D. (2021). Flexibility, failure and forging ahead. *Association for Middle Level Education.* https://www.amle.org/flexibility-failure-and-forging-ahead/

Torres, C. (2021). Rediscovering relationship-based learning. *Educational Leadership, 79*(1), 56–58. https://www.ascd.org/el/articles/rediscovering-relationship-based-learning

6

Resilience

Introduction

Over the last decade, I have frequently reminded myself that being me has served me well for a long time. As educators and scholars, we typically don't admit it, but we can feel insecure about our work, our progress, and our professional development. Although easier said than done, I truly believe that it is important for us to be ourselves, to believe in ourselves, and what we have to offer to our institutions, departments, and larger communities. Author Greg Spencer suggests, in his book *Reframing the Soul*, "Feeling at home does not mean all is well within our soul … it means we know who we are. We know our strengths and our weaknesses and we understand that spiritual and moral progress takes time" (2018, p. 162). Spencer recognizes that change can occur when we see our personal development as an inevitable process. His reminder encourages me to remain true to myself as I learn, adapt, and grow. Part of learning and growing professionally involves strengthening self-awareness around dispositions such as resilience. As educators continue to face challenges that test their resilience, the circumstances can be viewed as an opportunity to strengthen resilience. Tragedy and unexpected challenges can adversely encourage educators to build resilience and see others, both students and colleagues, with humanity and empathy (Paris, 2016).

DOI: 10.4324/9781003379539-6

I wholeheartedly believe that attributes such as grit, perseverance, and resilience are essential to not only equip pre-service teachers but to sustain them in long-term professional careers. As mentioned in previous chapters, teaching remains a complex and complicated profession (Korthagen et al., 2013; Palmer, 1998; Souers & Hall, 2019; Wormeli, 2015). Teaching is emotional and teachers are required to invest on multiple levels (Fallona & Canniff, 2013; Hill-Jackson et al., 2019) because teaching involves the heart, mind, and soul; the work of a teacher necessitates resiliency.

Teachers juggle a myriad of student personalities and needs. They focus on students' social and emotional health, everchanging standards and technology, curricular trends, differentiation, and academic needs. Teacher workloads and emotional responsibilities continue to shift as K-12 students and families face complicated circumstances and issues related to learning disabilities, language barriers, mental health and wellness, trauma, homelessness, and more. Today's teachers must dig deep within themselves when they commit to teaching. In order to elevate their professionalism and maintain and sustain a professional career, teachers must develop a toolbox of dispositions. As noted in earlier chapters of *Dispositions Are a Teacher's Greatest Strength,* teachers need a toolbox of intangible skills and postures in addition to traditional lesson plans, back to school night presentation plans, pedagogy, and team building activities (Hill-Jackson et al., 2019). Teaching necessitates fostering and cultivating prominent dispositions, such as resilience, so educators can tackle the scope of their professional responsibilities. Teachers must be able to solve problems, search for resources, and bounce back when the going gets tough.

Encountering the Unexpected

As a pre-service faculty member, several years ago my colleagues and I experienced an unusually hectic season full of unpredictable circumstances. We faced a host of unexpected disruptions to the academic calendar in 2017. Specifically in December, there was a feeling of heaviness when a powerful wild fire swept through my local community. Extreme smoke, unhealthy ash-filled air, and intense evacuations disrupted the small college campus where I worked. My own children experienced school closures as my college campus evacuated, faculty modified final exams, and my college community completed the semester's work remotely. Everyone in our larger community was either affected with an evacuation order, offered to host evacuees, or thoughtfully served friends in need. The fire's destruction stunned and stung our community as we entered the holiday season.

Once the smoke cleared after the holidays, the community made efforts to reset and find a sense of normalcy. Then, unfortunately and unexpectedly a few days into January, heavy rains soaked the county and mud literally buried parts of our beloved community in a matter of minutes. The fire had stopped burning in late December, but its impact and destruction to our foothills became ripe terrain for heavy rains, debris flow, and devastating mudslides. Once again, the community experienced uncertainty as friends and neighbors lost their lives, homes, and businesses. Utter devastation permeated our beautiful community to the core. In the months that followed, sporadic rains fueled additional disruptions with school closures and evacuations, power outages, and water quality issues. Just as one evacuation order lifted, another arrived, amplifying the community's pain and efforts to stay afloat. It became an increasing challenge to digest a breadth of emotions, hurt, and loss felt across the city.

There are far greater and more significant stories of deep hurt and personal loss to highlight; yet, I share my perspective in this chapter, hoping to underscore the physical and emotional impacts that each disruption had on the normal routine at my workplace, in local neighborhoods, and schools. Experiencing interruptions to my own teaching routine reminded me of the significant responsibility I have to develop and instill powerful dispositions like resilience in teacher training.

Pondering Resilience

Each year when I visit K-12 classrooms and supervise student teachers, I soak in the wide range of responsibilities teachers face. Smartphones, iPads, social media, anxiety, school safety, bullying, learning disabilities, lockdown drills, a shaky political climate, and *so* much more exacerbate the breadth of knowledge and skills new teachers must now possess. Parker Palmer (1998) skillfully named that teachers experience exuberance and joy in the classroom juxtaposed with moments of pain and perplexity. Using Palmer and the natural disasters in my community as a springboard, I chose to ponder the idea that if K-12 teachers can foster, develop, and model the disposition of resilience, the impact may also shape and equip K-12 students with resilience and courage for their own lives, especially when life throws unpredictable curve balls their way. I must acknowledge that while there are similarities between the dispositions of adaptability (explored in the previous chapter) and resilience, the disposition of resilience deserves its own platform and chapter.

Angela Duckworth describes grit as essential to goal setting and loving what you do. She names grit as a major predictor of success identifying resilience, intentionality, passion, and purpose as qualities that, when combined, cultivate grit. Furthermore, she suggests that a teacher needs to demonstrate assets such as perseverance and integrity to help themselves and their students identify work habits related to survival and growth (2016). Classifying these characteristics as assets of the heart (2018), Duckworth asserts that these assets are needed when a routine is disrupted or the struggles feel larger than ever. Remarkably, Duckworth raised her own children with a "Hard Thing Rule" that translates to choosing to do and stick with one hard thing or activity. Hayward extends Duckworth's approach suggesting that teachers should nurture grit in students so they become self-aware, willing to tell their own stories, and are able to create a culture for risk-taking (2015).

Similarly, Elena Aguilar's book *Outward: Cultivating Emotional Resilience in Educators* frames resilience in relation to how individuals weather the ups and downs of life and bounce back from them (2018, p. 2). Aguilar suggests that building resilience can serve to energize and fuel an individual's adaptability. I heard a similar approach firsthand when my husband and I attended our daughter's university orientation in 2018. The university's staff skillfully coached parents like us through a workshop focused on building resilience in college students. Presenters encouraged parents to come alongside their first-year college students to help them develop skills for decision-making as well as identify failures as part of growth (Boise State University, 2018). The message inspired parents to name their child's strengths and assets whenever challenges appeared. This encouragement affirmed my earlier resilience queries and also prompted me to ponder how my husband and I might demonstrate resilience to our daughter as first-time college parents. When considering resilience, it is important to remember that our weaknesses can actually become our strengths. As we focus on student assets, areas of growth for students do not need to convey weakness but instead can display great strength (Grant, 2023).

Curiously, I next discovered a link between resilience and the image of buoyancy. For me, buoyancy evokes an image of a buoy floating and bobbing up and down in the ocean; an ocean buoy is constructed to stay afloat even if it is pushed or pulled down in the sea; it is designed to rise to the surface again and again. The notion of buoyancy indicates lightness mingled with an ability to bounce back. Furthermore, resilience requires strength and flexibility. Soon after the previously mentioned community disasters, the Director of Counseling Services at my college shared that resilience can be regarded as a journey full of joy, pain, and setbacks (Nelson, 2018); he thoughtfully encouraged the college community to avoid avoiding and to face, name, and address the unexpected difficulties that the recent disasters caused in our community. Although these recommendations felt difficult to execute at the time, we were encouraged to approach the unexpected and its aftermath with buoyancy and intentionality.

As I continued to ponder the unexpected circumstances in my personal and professional life, I wondered how teachers remain buoyant, stay afloat, and thrive through the unexpected. I contemplated how I, a teacher of teachers, could prepare pre-service teachers to foster, model, and cultivate resilience when there is deep strain, tension, and anxiety embedded in the work. How could pre-service faculty like me, K-12 teachers, and school administrators prepare resilient teachers? In other words, how might we view resilience as an educator's strength so they are armed and ready to bounce back from the unexpected. It is interesting to note that resilient people often engage in difficult work over many years (Aguilar, 2018, p. 211); this finding has stuck with me. Educators must put in the time, commit to building personal and professional resilience, press on, and do the work. Fostering resilience with intention strengthens us while also helping others to become stronger.

In early 2018, after my community's natural disasters, I was able to connect with exceptional educators who demonstrated powerful and heroic examples of resilience. One such educator was forced to commute to and from her school on back roads for five hours a day because her normal route was blocked by the destructive mudslides. In order to restore routine and normalcy for elementary students, another local school's staff moved its classrooms to temporary campuses for several weeks after the natural disasters; these teachers showed up and demonstrated resilience far beyond their job descriptions. Likewise, a principal I know was forced to muster and maintain professional strength to support her teachers after a student passed away in one of the community's natural disasters. This school leader demonstrated amazing strength during unprecedented circumstances affirming research that shows that in unpredictable times, resilient school leaders are the glue to a resilient school community. It's revealing that schools are more likely to move forward from adversity if their school leadership demonstrates great resilience (New Leaders, 2022).

Beyond catastrophic events like the aforementioned, there are typical schools and predictable school days. I visit schools weekly to observe student teachers and see them and their cooperating teachers listening to students, encouraging them, and sharing struggles alongside them. Teachers convey and extend personal strength to students every day. They come alongside students wrestling with loss, a failed exam, a threat to their personal safety, or a bad dating relationship. Teachers, whether entrenched in extreme or ordinary circumstances, exhibit profound resilience firsthand when they make the choice to show up for day after day. Teachers choose to respond with intention, care, and kindness as they put students first in the midst of both predictable daily routines and remarkable challenges.

Resilience Recommendations

Exploring resilience yielded several recommendations for teachers with the goal that each strategy provides a starting point for teachers to cultivate and practice both resilience and courage in the classroom. I offer these practical suggestions: first, name the resilience we see in students. Acknowledging student assets can expose and strengthen students' skills and responses that lead to resilience. Teachers can make a conscious choice to foster a learning environment where student struggle is welcome and encouraged, especially when learning a new concept or topic. Framing mistakes as learning opportunities and practice as progress can generate greater student confidence and resilience. Thomas Hoerr goes so far as to suggest presenting explicit situations to students where they must problem solve nurtures skills of resilience (2013). Teachers can invite students to identify resilience as a strength when they problem solve. Educational psychologist Michele Borba's thinking aligns with this approach; she suggests that when an individual demonstrates moral courage, a person's confidence increases and actually builds resilience (2018). Practicing resilience as a teachable skill and habit develops an individual's problem-solving abilities. Read ahead to Chapter 11 for more on the disposition of courage.

A second recommendation for fostering resilience involves sharing stories of resilience. When teachers reflect and share personal experiences of resilience, they help prepare students for the real world (Hoerr, 2013); when this happens, a teacher's resilience, like a teacher's courage, becomes contagious. Teachers can present resilience as a focus for discussion with colleagues and students. In addition, school leaders can prompt teachers to share stories of resilience to empower others to persevere and stay the course. Souers and Hall's research upholds a similar recommendation that promotes teacher self-awareness as a form of self-care that establishes a culture of safety for students (2019). This research suggests that teachers should know themselves and acknowledge their past experiences and sources of influence in order to support students in intentional and proactive ways. Recognizing our own resilience as educators can serve as a powerful model to students and colleagues.

Lastly, to build resilience, I suggest carving out time for reflection. Teachers need time and space to take a walk, write in a journal, sit quietly, and breathe. Teachers can prioritize and find time to ponder and reflect on experiences when they have felt resilient or were forced to develop a resilient spirit. Ironically, the time I invested writing this chapter has helped me reflect and identify my own stories and experiences of personal and professional resilience. As described in earlier chapters of *Dispositions Are a Teacher's Greatest Strength*, reserving time in my daily calendar to reflect on dispositions, like resilience, becomes essential to my professional growth. In addition, creating space in meetings for teachers to reflect and ponder professional questions, both big and small, can also build teacher awareness and resilience. Teachers need authentic opportunities to name when they have had to dig deep to persevere, get through a tough time, bounce back, persevere, and ultimately flourish (Aguilar, 2018).

Resilience for Flourishing

A principal once shared with me that teachers need character, integrity, and heart skills to thrive in the profession. I sincerely hope that readers will recognize the impact of fostering the 13 dispositions in this book, including resilience. Although resilience is not easily seen or measured, educators can intentionally make efforts to nurture, convey, and practice resilience. I anticipate that teachers will foster resilience, in themselves and in their students, when they share personal stories and create classroom cultures where resilience is valued.

A former student, who is now a full-time teacher, provided a beautiful illustration of resilience when she sent my colleagues and me the following correspondence (Chambers, 2017):

> Today we got news that a student was killed in a car accident. This loss comes as a shock and with great sadness to me and the school. Heartbroken and unsure of how to carry out today, my mind goes back to my time with you. More than anything each of you taught me how to love, care, and provide for my students in the non-academic ways. To be mindful of the whole child and what they carry in their backpacks. Today, all our backpacks are full, heavy, and seemingly unbearable, but I am able to talk to my students about gratitude and about going home and hugging their parents tonight. I am impressed with the conversations that have come from this experience and I am encouraged by how well the students are handling it and supporting each other.

This heartfelt message demonstrates great resilience; moreover, the teacher's experience attests to the significant burden and necessity to foster resilience in ourselves and our students.

When I visited a high school classroom recently, I appreciated seeing a poster that named resilience as a habit of the heart: trying new things; being comfortable with the uncomfortable; adapting positively to adversity; identifying what's not working; and replacing what's not working with a positive behavior were attributes highlighted on the poster. Although resilience is often invisible to the eye, nurturing professional resilience in practice can bring long-term rewards and benefits to our professional lives, and our students' lives. More importantly, resilience is an inner strength that conveys great hope for the future. I enthusiastically suggest that we make resilience a priority for career sustainability and flourishing. I invite you to join me—buckle up, resilience is required.

Pause and Reflect

1. What personal and professional experiences have shaped your postures of resilience?
2. How have you responded to unexpected career circumstances with resilience and grace?
3. What other dispositions explored in *Dispositions Are a Teacher's Greatest Strength* draw out the disposition of resilience in you? Explain.
4. When you notice your own inner resilience, how do you feel? Do these feelings influence your attitudes or actions?
5. Have you made a conscious choice to develop inner resilience? Why or why not?

References

Aguilar, E. (2018). *Onward: Cultivating emotional resilience in educators.* Jossey-Bass.

Boise State University (2018). *Six strategies for building resilience [Handout].* Boise State University.

Borba, M. (2018). Nine competencies for teaching empathy. *Educational Leadership, 76*(2), 22–28. https://www.ascd.org/el/articles/nine-competencies-for-teaching-empathy

Chambers, J. (2017). Personal communication.

Duckworth, A. (2016). *Grit: The power of passion and perseverance.* Simon and Schuster.

Duckworth, A. (2018). Grit and the greater good: A conversation with Angela Duckworth. *Educational Leadership, 76*(2), 40–45. https://www.ascd.org/search?ascd_master%5Bquery%5D=grit%20and%20the%20greater%20good

Fallona, C., & Canniff, J. (2013). Nurturing a moral stance in teacher education. In M. N. Sanger, & R. D. Osguthrope (Eds.), *The moral work of teaching and teacher education* (pp. 75–91). Teachers College Press.

Grant, A. (2023). Shouldn't these things be obvious? Instagram [@adamgrant]. https://www.instagram.com/adamgrant/

Hayward, M. O. (2015). Got grit? Leading and teaching for success. *Association for Middle Level Education Magazine, 3*(3), 24–26.

Hill-Jackson, V., Hartlep, N. D., & Stafford, D. (2019). *What makes a star teacher: 7 dispositions that support student learning.* ASCD.

Hoerr, T. (2013). *Fostering grit: How do I prepare my students for the real world.* ACSD Arias.

Korthagen, F. A. J., Kim, Y. M., & Greene, W. L. (2013). *Teaching and learning from within: A core reflection approach to quality and inspiration in education.* Routledge.

Nelson, E. (2018). *Cultivating resilience: Coming to terms with life's inevitable difficulty.* Presented at Westmont College, Santa Barbara, California.

New Leaders (2022). *The relationship between resilient leaders and resilient students.* New Leaders. https://www.newleaders.org/blog/the-relationship-between-resilient-leaders-and-resilient-students

Palmer, P. (1998). *The courage to teach. Exploring the inner landscape of a teacher's life.* Jossey-Bass.

Paris, J. (2016). *Teach from the heart: Pedagogy as spiritual practice.* Cascade Books.

Souers, K. V. M., & Hall, P. (2019). *Relationship, responsibility and regulation: Trauma- invested practices for fostering resilient learners.* ASCD.

Spencer, G. (2018). *Reframing the soul: How words transform our faith.* Leafwood Publishers.

Wormeli (2015). The seven habits of highly affective teachers. *Educational Leadership, 73*(2), 10–15. https://www.ascd.org/el/articles/the-seven-habits-of-highly-affective-teachers

7

Gratitude

Introduction

Exploring the disposition of gratitude sparked my curiosity for how educators can use gratitude as a tool to strengthen teacher practice. Expressing appreciation—whether to a student, parent, or colleague—serves as a small, yet mighty gesture, that reminds others of their worth, value, and importance. The reverse is true as well; receiving appreciative words from others reminds us of our own personal value.

Psychologist Adam Grant recognizes that gratitude expressions make people feel good and makes them stronger (2022). There is significant professional value in expressing gratitude and receiving gratitude, so much so that in the last decade, gratitude has become a vibrant research field that reveals the "feel good" benefits that Grant acknowledges as well as significant health benefits. Research suggests that simple gestures of gratitude increase personal happiness especially when the gestures are unexpected (Howells, 2012); efforts to model and share gratitude and appreciation for others, attract and connect people. In addition, a person who demonstrates gratitude conveys an authentic readiness for appreciation and an eagerness to return kindness.

Results from a 2019 European study of over 500 college students reveals that the greatest predictor of psychological well-being is gratitude; hope, optimism, and life satisfaction

DOI: 10.4324/9781003379539-7

follow as additional predictors (Kardas et al., 2019). Since gratitude is typically associated with positive emotions and behaviors, developing, implementing, and expressing gratitude can benefit teachers and students in a variety of ways. Demonstrating gratitude can take many forms: thank you notes, emails, verbal expressions of thanks, as well as inner gratitude practices like prayer, mindfulness, or meditation. These expressions are both practical and authentic. Offering appreciation for or to another individual can create an inner feeling that far outweighs the substance of what was shared. Likewise, gratitude journaling or simply writing down what we are grateful for actually improves an individual's personal happiness. Moreover, expressing gratitude through letter writing, whether direct or subtle, touches others because of the thoughtful intention behind the letter writing. Letters of gratitude can actually increase positivity and decrease stress levels (Wilson, 2016, p. 8). Intentional expressions of gratitude like the aforementioned communicate value from one person to another (Sima, 2022), while at the same time heighten our personal self-awareness of gratitude. Preparing our inner self for gratitude influences how we function in the classroom *and* how gratitude transfers from teacher to students.

With gratitude, sincerity is key. When expressions of gratitude are artificial or inauthentic, gratitude can be misconstrued as toxic optimism. It can be dismissed as too "touchy-feely," fake, or even sugar-coated. Effective expressions of thanks must be genuine, such that students, parents, and colleagues can authentically engage in building a classroom culture of gratitude together. When teachers incorporate the disposition of gratitude into their daily practice, the expressions and actions strengthen the classroom's ethos and students' learning. "Attention to our inner attitude gives us access to the aspect of teacher presence where we are aware of the impact of our thoughts and actions on those we teach" (Howells, 2012, p. 87). Gratitude in our classrooms is a gift; it increases engrossment and engagement in learning, and it enlarges students' perspectives of and for learning (Wilson & Foster, 2018).

Gratitude's Ripple Effects

As mentioned in earlier chapters, my pre-service program places heavy emphasis on four dispositions, one of which is *gratitude*. Our program's expectation is that students develop as grateful professionals who "display a humble and appreciative demeanor dedicated to the service of others" (Department of Education Dispositions Statement, 2021, p. 5). Keeping this expectation in mind, our faculty team feels that it is important to prepare student teachers for the reality that some K-12 students and even some teacher colleagues are not enthusiastic about school. Rather than looking to recognize what is going well as a K-12 student or teacher, these individuals may choose to look for the next best thing to complain about. Unfortunately, negativity or a lack of gratitude can actually become counterproductive to one's work and work environment (Rath & Clifton, 2015). First lady Martha Washington's famous message to learn from experience, whether joyful or difficult, can remind us to focus on our dispositions and not our circumstances (Foster, 2015). Washington urges individuals to demonstrate gratitude and view gratitude as an asset. Consider the age-old full or empty bucket theory that recognizes people with a full bucket have a positive outlook, whereas people with an empty bucket can undermine a positive outlook. Choosing a full or empty bucket can positively influence our health, joy, and productivity (Rath & Clifton, 2015). Developing a grateful disposition can energize us, whereas possessing an ungrateful disposition can deplete us. It becomes difficult to build a habit of gratitude when we choose to gossip, blame, or complain about others. Alternatively, as we develop relationships with colleagues and students, we can intentionally choose to convey gratitude through our words, attitudes, and gestures. Now, don't get me wrong, teachers need occasions to share woes and frustrations because teaching is extremely difficult work; teachers need opportunities to share their struggles in productive and healthy ways with trusted colleagues and mentors. Author Greg Spencer recognizes that routinely engaging in gratitude practices can elevate individuals during times of stress and uncertainty. Spencer urges us to examine the past with gratitude, even our past struggles, so we can find appreciation in our circumstances. Gratitude can change our perspective and how we view the future (2018). In light of this, I suggest we cultivate authentic gratitude: gratitude that can persist with honesty and hope even during our most challenging teaching struggles.

Research shows that when youth intentionally practice gratitude, their actions affect their grades, academic achievement, and emotions; gratitude is worth a teacher's time and attention and there are numerous ways to make and develop gratitude as a daily practice (McKibben, 2022). Referring back to her earlier research on gratitude, educator Sarah McKibben offers a variety of techniques to foster gratitude in the classroom: appreciate kind acts with gratitude, pair students for cooperation, encourage service learning, and model gratitude (2013). Her last recommendation, to model gratitude, resonates with me. In my experience, teachers who practice gratitude encourage their students to follow suit, *and* teachers often feel greater job satisfaction. Once individuals observe others modeling habits [such as gratitude] they will be more open to what is being taught and modeled (Covey, 2008, p. 214). For instance, if a teacher routinely expresses gratitude to students after a fieldtrip or class discussion, students will become more open to the habit and their teacher. Or if a teacher habitually reframes a negative circumstance as an opportunity, students will learn from and mimic their teacher's behavior. Engaging in intentional expressions of gratitude can prompt a shift in mindset for both students and teachers.

Practicing gratitude reaps benefits that impact learning and attitudes for learning while also reducing stress levels for both teachers and students (Wilson, 2016). Practicing gratitude can even help students with their mental health. One advocate for gratitude recommends three strategies to develop appreciation: (1) look for gratitude (like we are doing in this chapter); (2) model gratitude; and (3) strive to foster a grateful community (Yomantas, 2022). Finding time to ponder and name what we are grateful for as well as where we find gratitude can fill us up and improve students' mindsets. Additionally, giving students opportunities to recognize what they are grateful for awakens the disposition of gratitude in them.

Investing in gratitude practices also fosters an individual's self-awareness. When teachers take time to name and share what they are grateful for, they are often able to reset or reframe. Author and psychologist Brené Brown notes that practicing and internalizing gratitude alters our mindsets and actions (2018). Similarly, Hollywood actor Michael J. Fox finds gratitude every day, even as he has lived with Parkinson's Disease for over 30 years. In a recent interview, Fox notes that gratitude cultivates hope and optimism in him (2023). Fox is an extreme example of an individual who recognizes gratitude in the face of challenging circumstances; yet, his humble ability to seek and name gratitude in the middle of deep suffering is both admirable and inspiring. Author Ken Shigematsu captures a similar perspective in his book, *Survival Guide for the Soul:* "When we become people who give thanks for what happened in the past, we will also become people who savor the present moment" (2018, p. 112). Gratitude requires and inspires reflection; likewise, according to Shigematsu, turning our attention to the experiences, struggles, and joys we have encountered in the past, both professionally and personally, shines a light on gratitude and its impact on the future.

Gratitude Shines

As with many of the other dispositions in this book, gratitude comes naturally for some teachers; yet, others must intentionally work to foster it. Even so, gratitude can be practiced and learned; when we intentionally practice expressing gratitude, we can begin to form habits of gratitude. Gratitude circles where a class or group of students sit together and share stories of gratitude, as well as intentional pair-share time where two students name what they are grateful for are two practical strategies that can help teachers and students nurture inner gratitude. In addition, when I visit K-12 classrooms, I regularly notice gratitude walls and bulletin boards filled with gratitude trees, post-it notes of appreciation, or gratitude poems. These tangible displays of gratitude allow K-12 students (and teachers) to identify postures and expressions of appreciation that extend beyond traditional holidays such as Thanksgiving and Valentine's Day; the displays gently remind both teachers and students to be grateful throughout the school day.

An additional approach to fostering gratitude occurs when teachers pose questions to students: "What did you enjoy about this book?" or "What did you appreciate about this biology lab?" When teachers link student learning and gratitude, they invite students to reflect as well as engage in gratitude routines. Breathing and focusing is another approach for teachers and students to develop gratitude (Wilson & Foster, p. 6). For this practice, individuals are invited to breathe in deeply, reflect, and examine their attitudes. Engaging in breathing and focusing exercises nurture an individual's heart and spirit. Likewise, I find that lists can be a practical way to nurture the disposition of gratitude. When I was home with my family during the early days of the pandemic, I recall pulling out chart paper to start a gratitude list in the front hallway of our house. I asked my children and husband to add to the list each week. We recorded simple expressions of gratitude: meals, moments of laughter, favorite beach walks, and even doorstep grocery deliveries. Our list grew from one page, to two, and ultimately to eight pages; the list became a visible reminder of all the heartfelt moments of gratitude that brought my family inner gladness during the pandemic. In addition, the list helped me realize the things that I had previously taken for granted professionally before the pandemic, whether it was casual interactions with colleagues in our office hallway or stimulating interactions with students in person after class, the pandemic produced space for thoughtful reflection and increased gratitude. In addition, practicing gratitude can be a pathway to joy *and* sharing gratitude, especially during challenging times, can cultivate inner joy (Kanold, 2021). You can read more about the disposition of joy in Chapter 13.

Through the years in pre-service education, I discovered that the students who feel the most challenging for me professionally, often express the most gratitude. In full transparency, whether they are first-year undergraduates or student teachers nearing the end of our pre-service program, these students sometimes push my buttons and can test my patience. Gratefully, I haven't interacted with very many students like this, but as you know, when students test our patience, they typically stand out and whether we like it or not, we remember them clearly. In my experience, these students may be unable to see the long-term benefits of their daily efforts or they may not be meeting their true professional potential. Ironically, over time, these students will surprise me—with a text message, a note of gratitude, or an invitation for coffee. Even as I write this chapter, I received several text messages from former student teachers. One former student in particular struggled to see beyond his immediate circumstances as a student teacher. James (a pseudonym) routinely felt overwhelmed, buried in paperwork, and behind in his grading. Ironically, several years into his teaching career, James reached out to me via a text message to express sincere thanks for some advice I had given him when he was in our pre-service program. When I initially gave James the advice, I remember wondering if my suggestions even resonated with him; yet years later, his thoughtful text message was an authentic display of gratitude. Knowing that the advice I shared with James made an impact years later warms my heart, makes me grateful for James, as well as the work I hold dear. The text exchange with James reminds me of the importance of gratitude and its ripple effects. Engaging with a former student at the grocery store, having a former student text or call for advice, or reading about a former student's professional accomplishments in the newspaper stirs gratitude in me: gratitude for my vocation, appreciation for the relationships and interactions, as well as the long-term privilege and perspective I gain looking back. Gratitude can help us remember that the way we treat our students shapes their actions and character well beyond the time we have with them in our classrooms (Johnson, 2015).

As is true with other dispositions (for example, curiosity in Chapter 2 and resilience in Chapter 6), practicing gratitude helps teachers learn the habit of gratitude so they can eventually adopt the disposition as a natural behavior. My faculty colleague, Laura (a pseudonym), became an expert on gratitude. For almost a decade, she researched, modeled, and lived out the disposition of gratitude across our college campus. Her professional actions and attitudes habitually overflowed with gratitude. Remarkably, Laura was able to find the positive in most every situation and was consistently able to frame (and even reframe) a disappointing circumstance with a grateful heart. Laura even initiated the weekly practice of asking her student teachers to reflect on the former week and then complete their "3 G's": first naming what they were *grateful* for; secondly identifying how they had demonstrated *grit* during the week; and lastly, she asked students to set a specific *goal* for growth. Thanks to Laura's example, I learned that cultivating gratitude enlarges our lens for appreciation and expands our teacher toolbox. Laura's consistent efforts to model gratitude as well as her commitment to internalize gratitude permeated through her teaching, collegial relationships, and scholarship. Her ability to literally live out the disposition of gratitude reinforced the power of nurturing this core disposition in practice.

Gratitude's Ripple Effects

Gratitude practices create ripple effects; gratitude energizes teachers, strengthens practice, and fosters greater connections between teachers with students. When educators demonstrate gratitude, our students see it and feel it. Educator Owen Griffith notes that when a student expresses gratitude for things such as homework or things at home, his classroom culture improves and gratitude grows (2014). Whether gratitude expressions are shared in the form of gratitude journals, gifts, or notes, they can improve the lives of students and teachers. Just as a teacher incorporates art or music into a lesson, creating space for gratitude reaps classroom rewards. Explicitly sharing gratitude with an intentional and specific "thank you" makes an impact. Thanking a student for a creative response to a homework writing prompt or expressing thoughtful appreciation for a student's positive behavior can empower the student. Gratitude practices genuinely uplift student recipients and inspire increased confidence in them (Griffith, 2014).

Many years ago, my husband Chris, who is a junior high school teacher, started a tradition in our home. Chris prompted a routine group of dinner guests to share "a story of the day" and through the years, this prompt has repeatedly elicited stories from guests that produced laughter, humor, tears, *and* gratitude (in full professional disclosure, the stories are shared with professional tact, confidentiality, and anonymity). As educators, most of us can easily share more than one "story of the day"; however, finding and designating time to do so often feels challenging. Carving out time to reflect and share professional stories with others can stimulate gratitude in us. And whether my "story of the day" involves students, colleagues, or myself, I find that with each story, my attitude and hunger for gratitude deepens for the subjects of my stories and the profession I cherish.

When I connect with teachers in the field, I routinely ask them to share how they implement dispositions in practice in their own classrooms. When I ask about the disposition of gratitude, they often tell me about the gratitude circles mentioned earlier in this chapter. They also speak about affirming and valuing colleagues with words and expressions of gratitude. Asking students to reflect on and name their high and low, or their rose and thorn from the week, is a tried-and-true strategy that fosters gratitude; the activity functions to highlight gratitude, demonstrate gratitude, and develop increased student and teacher self-awareness for gratitude. In the same way, when student teachers complete their full-time clinical placements, I ask them to revisit their initial goals for displaying gratitude in the classroom. Helping student teachers recognize the idealism in their initial goals juxtaposed with the reality of how they actually demonstrated gratitude is enlightening; student teachers often recognize that when they implement regular feedback and suggestions from faculty supervisors or cooperating teachers, they are better able to convey a deep and sincere form of gratitude that feels meaningful. In addition, implementing specific feedback from cooperating teachers or faculty supervisors truly honors the time, suggestions, and investment given to a student teacher. My student teachers are generally grateful people, but when my feedback is explicit and thoughtful, I find that they express increased gratitude. Furthermore, when teachers feel inner gratitude and when they authentically express gratitude to their students, students are impacted in positive ways.

Since my first year of teaching, I have kept a "smile file" full of notes and cards from students. Whenever I receive a note from a student, I feel an immense sense of in-the-moment gratitude and warmth toward the student. My heart stirs, fills up, and I am reminded of the interactions between the student and me. More profoundly, I am reminded of the reason I chose to teach which then prompts me to reflect on my professional journey. Similarly, when I experience a challenging work day, I often choose to open up my "smile file" and read a few notes to feel refreshed and inspired once again. When practiced, the disposition of gratitude is truly a gift that generates and radiates more gratitude. As educators, I suggest that we search with eagerness for opportunities to express gratitude and pay it forward.

Pause and Reflect

1. What insights or new perspectives did you gain from reading this chapter?
2. What does your posture of appreciation look like in your classroom? How might you routinely offer authentic expressions of gratitude to your students?
3. When you share or express gratitude to or for others, how do you feel inside?
4. When you are the recipient of another individual's gratitude from a student, administrator, colleague, or parent, how do you feel? Consider how you can pay this feeling forward.
5. How can the disposition of gratitude positively propel you forward as a professional?

References

Brown, B. (2018). *Dare to lead*. Random House.

Covey, S. R. (2008). *The leader in me*. Free Press.

Department of Education Dispositions Statement (2021). In *Westmont Department of Education Teacher Credential Program Handbook 2022-2023*, p. 5. https://www.westmont.edu/sites/default/files/ users/user451/Teacher%20Credential%20Handbook%20for%20 Printing_0.pdf

Foster, F. S. (2015). *Feather Schwartz Foster Blog*. https://featherschwartz foster.blog/2015/09/21/martha-washingtons-disposition/

Fox, M. J. (2023). *Michael J. Fox discusses gratitude* [Interview]. CBS This Morning.

Grant, A. (2022). *The research: "Gratitude expressions improve teammates' cardiovascular stress responses."* Instagram [@adamgrant]. https:// www.instagram.com/adamgrant/

Griffith, O. M. (2014). *Gratitude: A powerful tool for your classroom*. Edutopia. https://www.edutopia.org/blog/gratitude-powerful- tool-for-classroom-owen-griffith

Howells, K. (2012). *Gratitude in education: A radical view*. Sense Publishers.

Johnson, L. (2015). *Teaching outside the box: How to grab your students by their brains* (2nd ed.). Jossey-Bass.

Kanold, T. D. (2021). *Soul! Fulfilling the promise of your professional life as a teacher and leader*. Solution Tree Press.

Kardas, F., Cam, Z., Esikisu, M., & Gelibolu, S. (2019). Gratitude, hope, optimism and life satisfaction as predictors of psychological well- being. *Eurasian Journal of Education Research, 82*, 81–100. https:// doi.org/10.14689/ejer.2019.82.5

McKibben, S. (2013). Tapping into the power of gratitude. *Educational Leadership 55*(11). https://www.ascd.org/el/articles/tapping-into- the-power-of-gratitude

McKibben, S. (2022). Getting back to gratitude. *ACSD Blog*. https://www.ascd. org/blogs/getting-back-to-gratitude?utm_campaign=Express- FY2023&utm_medium=email&_hsmi=235176685&_hsenc= p2ANqtz-_o7GLcg1EJYKbmT3JCjf0vojCgwCNrUdO-J4o1ogNv1h_ LIJgsCpFn2t7ZH1F39e5oGnqMaDhEFPg-EvSmofdVpz853g&utm_ content=235176683&utm_source=hs_email

Rath, T., & Clifton, D. O. (2015). *How full is your bucket?* Gallup Press.

Shigematsu, K. (2018). *Survival guide for the soul*. Zondervan.

Sima, R. (2022). Showing gratitude is good for all of us, so why don't we give thanks more? *The Washington Post*. https://www.washingtonpost.com/search/?query=Sima%2C+Showing+gratitude

Spencer, G. (2018). *Reframing the soul*. Leafwood Publishers.

Wilson, J. T. (2016). Brightening the mind: The impact of practicing gratitude on focus and resilience in learning. *Journal of the Scholarship of Teaching and Learning, 16*(4), 1–13. https://doi.org/10.14434/josotl.vl6i4.19998

Wilson, J., & Foster, R. (2018). The power, structure, and practice of gratitude in education: A demonstration of epistemology and empirical research working together. *International Christian Community of Teacher Educators, 13*(1), 4–11.

Yomantas, E. (2022). Weaving gratitude into the fabric of everyday learning. *Association for Middle Level Education*. https://www.amle.org/weaving-gratitude-into-the-fabric-of-everyday-learning/

8

Encouragement

Encouragement in Different Contexts

Chapter 8 shines a light on how to practically pursue and develop the disposition of encouragement. Encouragement from a teacher takes many forms, including seemingly small acts such as enthusiastically high-fiving a student after a spelling test, or patiently sitting and reviewing flashcards with a student. Notably, the disposition of encouragement becomes a crucial motivator for students when challenging circumstances such as trauma or grief occur; teachers selflessly and faithfully walk alongside students when they face trials and stress (Minkel, 2020). As addressed in previous chapters of *Dispositions Are a Teacher's Greatest Strength*, developing and modeling dispositions necessitate time, care, vulnerability, and empathy. Instances where I have supported a student through the loss of a family member, or assisted a student that has been ill for an extended time period, or even comforted a student when they learned about their parents' divorce, have pushed me to understand more about the disposition of encouragement.

I find it intriguing that the word *encouragement* contains the word *courage*; encouraging students requires courage. Courage is defined as "mental or moral strength to venture, persevere, and withstand danger, fear, or difficulty" (Merriam-Webster, 2023). I must also point out that the root of the word courage is *cor* or *cour* that means heart (Merriam-Webster, 2023) which leads

DOI: 10.4324/9781003379539-8

me to wonder if the disposition of encouragement serves as a conduit to the other dispositions explored in this book. Looking ahead, Chapter 10 will explore the disposition of courage in greater detail. In the meantime, as we consider encouragement, it is important to acknowledge the negative impacts of discouragement that teachers often feel. Teachers who feel discouragement may experience despair or may feel demoralized. Teachers are not immune to these feelings so finding pathways for teachers to feel encouraged as well as share encouragement feels like a noble pursuit.

I don't need to remind you that as teachers, we teach more than our content. Although we are invested in the curriculum we teach, we also feel a great responsibility to support our students emotionally. We know that teachers traditionally teach because they care deeply, want to inspire, and empower students; therefore, contemplating how we can sincerely encourage students can help teachers serve them well and hopefully empower students as learners and individuals. Ultimately, teachers want to develop students—as creative thinkers, critical thinkers, and problem solvers. Teachers also strive to develop students' social and emotional intelligence; cultivating habits of encouragement, both implicitly and explicitly, can strengthen teacher practice and build confidence in students. Classrooms are contexts where students are expected to learn and progress and K-12 education, in particular, is designed to shape students' connections with others so they contribute to society (Ryan et al., 2016). Educator Clifton L. Taulbert affirms this thinking noting that educators teach and serve children because of the moral aspects of education that prepare students to play a contributing role in society (2006, p. 119). Thus, the disposition of encouragement becomes integral to students' success and motivation so they can pursue and achieve their goals. Focusing on the disposition of encouragement in the classroom benefits students because a teacher's active and consistent presence, actions, words, and postures empower students.

After spending over three decades in classrooms, I find that students like to learn, but motivated students *love* to learn and they thoroughly embrace learning. Teachers know that motivation impacts student achievement, student perceptions, student goals, student attitudes, and student motivation (Rowell & Hong, 2013). For most teachers, stimulating a student's intrinsic motivation serves as the preferred motivational method over extrinsic motivation that focuses on rewards; however, for students that do not naturally find learning enjoyable, extrinsic motivation can play a distinct role in learning and can often help guide academic, social and emotional behaviors. Seeking to understand what motivates students helps all educators, teachers, principals, counselors, and superintendents, to encourage and support students as individuals. Educators can differentiate their acts and displays of encouragement by seeking to understand what will motivate and inspire students individually and collectively.

Presence as Encouragement

Charlie Mackesy's beautiful book, *The Boy, the Mole, the Fox and the Horse* captures the essence of presence when one of the book's characters, the mole, recommends to his friend, the boy, that he find a quiet space to breathe and focus in order to be present (2019, p. 32). Committing to this type of presence, to finding space to be in the moment with students serves as modest and steady encouragement to both students and teachers. It isn't a secret that students thrive when they are known, seen, and welcomed by a teacher. Students are drawn to teachers. Most often, students want to please their teachers, tell them stories, or ask them for advice. I have observed K-12 students pose questions such as, "How many kids do you have?" or "Can I tell you what I did this weekend?" or "What do you think about my topic for this project?" When students initiate inquiry in this way, a teacher's presence, posture, and response matters. If the teacher is in a hurry or is unable to answer, the student won't feel encouraged, but if the teacher pauses to listen to the student's question, the student will feel cared for. Students ultimately want to connect and engage in relationship with their teachers. Teacher presence and student accessibility to their teacher make a significant impact; there is encouraging power and subtle messaging in a teacher's presence when they show up for students. Students look forward to seeing their teachers each day and they are typically disappointed when there is a substitute teacher or a change in routine. A teacher's consistent presence conveys welcome, security, safety, and encouragement. For students, knowing what to expect each day provides additional physical and emotional security. Students appreciate knowing that their teacher (or team of teachers) will greet them at the door each morning and will guide them through the day's learning activities. And teachers know that how we teach matters but how we make students feel matters more.

Recent research identifies a direct connection between the body, the brain, and well-being, specific to faculty in higher education. The research also acknowledges that teaching is a profession where teachers bring their whole selves (Coleman & Dotter, 2020, p. 19). As a result, it can feel challenging to separate a teacher's person-ness and individuality from their professional teacher-ness. Teaching often consumes teachers' personal and professional lives and becomes a way of being; teaching is part of an educator's DNA. For this reason, mindfulness practices can help individuals generate contentment, maintain balance, and demonstrate sincere presence (Coleman & Dotter, 2020, p. 21). Moreover, presence, both consistent physical and mental presence, can serve as encouragement to students and even to teachers themselves. We know that the brain works like a muscle because it can be molded and shaped (Jensen, 2008); and mindfulness practices such as deep breathing can increase brain function, lower stress, and enhance academic performance (Coleman & Dotter, 2020). When teachers recognize how and when we are mentally present as professionals, we can be poised to encourage others.

Be a Student's Champion

A team of researchers recently examined the Program for International Student Assessment (PISA) scores and the relationship between students' perceptions of teachers' behaviors and reading achievement (Dadandi & Dadandi, 2022). Their compelling study reveals that students' reading enjoyment and self-efficacy contribute to students' reading achievement and the desire to read more. The study argues that teachers' encouraging behaviors—such as asking questions to encourage participation, or prompting students to share their perspectives about reading content, further promotes self-efficacy and reader success. Thus, teacher behaviors that convey valuing the whole student, whether the student is a college undergraduate or a budding first grader, encourage the student. Recognizing students' assets and interests also serves as a powerful method for increasing the self-efficacy of learners. I so appreciate a colleague who routinely proclaims that teachers need to be every student's champion; a teacher-champion invests in, believes in, and regularly encourages their students.

Remarkably, when teachers, schools, and administrators engaged with students online during the pandemic, juggled timelines for re-opening, and ran classes in person with masks, they discovered new methods for encouraging students. Of particular interest, elementary teacher Jessica Egbert, offered thoughtful advice to new and veteran teachers during the pandemic: (1) cheer for students; (2) praise students; (3) read aloud to students; and (4) validate students' challenges (2020, pp. 23–25). Egbert's reminders aren't new to educators; however, they affirm the importance of employing a variety of strategies that encourage students in a medley of ways. Egbert's modest suggestions inspire educators like me to make intentional efforts to authentically affirm and support students as a means of encouragement.

Post-pandemic, students are in need of an extra dose of encouragement—especially when they need to ask for their teacher's help (AMLE, 2021). Displaying encouragement to students, especially with an added dose of patience, is essential because increasingly students need time to think and process before they are ready to ask for a teacher's help. According to the Association for Middle Level Education, teachers may need to offer explicit and repeated support to students before they feel safe or are willing to accept a teacher's help (2021). In addition, offering creative pathways for students to solicit help can protect them from added angst when all they are really looking for is support. Curiously, my undergraduate students have shared that asking faculty for help can feel intimidating; therefore, creating a classroom culture where students of all ages can feel safe and encouraged makes asking for a teacher's help more attainable. Additionally, as addressed in earlier chapters of *Dispositions Are a Teacher's Greatest Strength*, creating and cultivating space for mistake-making and risk-taking matters too. When students feel secure, they are able to seek help and resources, *and* they build confidence. Explicitly encouraging students amidst their mistakes and failures can foster hope and resilience in them when they feel discouraged or confused. Refer back to Chapter 6 for more details on the disposition of resilience and look ahead to Chapter 12 to learn more about the disposition of hope.

Encouragement for Empowerment

I distinctly remember a time when a student teacher named Heather (a pseudonym) felt challenged when she was asked to make connections between her discipline and literacy. Educators know that literacy weaves through all of the disciplines we teach and today's educators are expected to be teachers of literacy even if they don't teach language arts or English. In Heather's case, I came alongside her and took the time to work through expectations and some tangible examples for how she could incorporate literacy into her lessons. Afterward, she felt encouraged to link vocabulary, writing exercises, and reading excerpts to her content. Simply taking some time to meet Heather where she was at encouraged her and she was able to move past her initial confusion with positivity. Moreover, developing and accessing a toolbox of strategies to encourage students like Heather can remind educators to take time to communicate care, spark inspiration, and nurture student confidence.

Similarly, demonstrating encouragement can also empower students' sense of agency as well as motivate them to be their best selves. Encouraging students to value who they are so that they know that they are an esteemed part of a classroom community reminds us of the profoundly meaningful work we get to engage in as educators. In addition, we can encourage students to listen to their own inner voices, provide space for them to develop their voices, and take advantage of classroom instances where they can foster their self-awareness (Taulbert, 2006, p. 104). Helping students to capitalize on their strengths, as well as to grow their weaknesses, encourages them; additionally, recognizing students' assets, their diverse intelligences and their learning styles conveys encouragement and reinforces teacher and student connections. Students need a teacher's encouragement to recognize their strengths as well as realize that their weaknesses are often areas of strength. I noticed this type of encouragement when I read about two junior high school teachers who seek to elevate students' voices. The team of teachers incorporates poetry into their teaching and although their students find writing poetry quite challenging, one student in particular recognizes that with time, practice, and consistent encouragement she felt a sense of permission to take risks to continue writing poetry (Simpson & Millikan, 2023). This relevant example encourages me to remember—that when we encounter students that won't try writing a poem, or won't attempt to complete a math problem, or won't read aloud unless they feel supported—that encouragement motivates and empowers students. What's more, finding ways to develop and practice using words and acts of encouragement can increase student motivation, achievement, and confidence. When teachers encourage students, we create space—a small window—for authentic hope and motivation to exist. It can feel challenging to encourage students when they are unmotivated or are surrounded by difficult circumstances, yet, I find that each time I see a student smile in response to a few words or a small act of encouragement, it energizes me.

Who is Encouraging Teachers?

I'd be remiss to arrive at the end of this chapter without asking the question, "Who is encouraging teachers?" With falling teacher retention rates and systematic pressures, it is crucial for school leaders to consider what can be done to encourage and empower teachers. Typically, when teachers feel valued and respected, there is greater retention and increased school stability; appreciating teachers trickles down directly to students and benefits students. So, as we ponder the disposition of encouragement and reflect on our work as encouragers, I hope that we experience professional renewal and further incentive to encourage others.

Teaching is often referred to as a helping profession. I appreciate this simple phrase because it serves as a gentle reminder to help and care for students. As teachers we care deeply about our students, however, we routinely minimize our personal needs to attend to our students' needs. Author Steven Glazer recognizes that while educators bring care to their students, they also need to grant themselves permission to do inner work and care for themselves (1999 p. 249). Educator Chase Mielke upholds this conclusion recognizing that self-care is selfish; yet, teachers must challenge traditional norms by first taking care of themselves and then their students (2021). Mielke's admonition reminds me to appreciate my colleagues who regularly suggest that I rest and recharge my professional batteries. I find that when colleagues pose thoughtful questions or suggestions, they are offering me encouragement to consider my own self-care choices as well as replenish my energy so that I can be my best self for my students.

Despite the pressures and complexities of teaching, teachers haven't stopped caring about teaching students. A recent study focused on teacher turnover concludes that teachers continue to provide an "abundance of dedication—care, heart, and hope." Furthermore, while there are numerous aspects of education that need to be addressed to retain teachers, simply recognizing, expressing gratitude for, and encouraging teachers should be a strong consideration to improve teacher retention (Pendola et al., 2023). Recognizing teachers in ways that they appreciate benefits teachers; knowing how to encourage teachers impacts their perceptions and attitudes and ultimately affects students' perceptions and attitudes. An additional study examined teacher and principal perceptions. Participants revealed, through a variety of surveys and interviews, an extensive list of positive principal behaviors and attitudes that teachers genuinely appreciate

(Richards, 2007). A follow-up study by the same researcher next unpacked teacher perceptions about the previous study's findings noting five principal behaviors that teachers appreciated: (1) principals value and respect teachers; (2) principals support teachers with student discipline; (3) principals have an open-door policy; (4) principals are trustworthy and fair; and (5) principals support parents and teachers. Although these research findings focus primarily on teacher perceptions regarding what they value in principal behaviors, results also reveal ways principals and school leaders can offer encouragement to teachers. For example, when a principal recognizes a teacher's effort publicly or privately, or leaves an encouraging note, or asks how a teacher is doing, a teacher feels encouraged and valued (Richards, 2007).

In an ideal world, all educators would feel optimal levels of encouragement from their districts, administrators, colleagues, and larger school communities; however, in reality, it becomes essential for teachers to seek out their own support from colleagues, mentors, and friends. Informal book groups, after school social gatherings, or even taking a campus walk with a colleague at lunchtime can serve as forms of encouragement for teachers. These groups, interactions, and gatherings can happen organically during the academic year or they may be formally introduced by school leaders or district initiatives. Teacher support groups, whether online or in person, can serve as additional places and spaces where teachers can experience encouragement and build relational connections in the workplace.

I urge readers to contemplate how we can encourage students, colleagues, *and* ourselves generously. One of my student teachers, Sarah (a pseudonym), used to write, "I've got this!" in bold letters on the top of her weekly lesson plans. This short phrase served as motivation for Sarah to build her confidence, do her best, and become her best teacher-self. All educators, whether they are teachers, administrators, or higher education faculty members, need encouragement. Because nurturing skills of encouragement influences our professional perceptions and attitudes in the classroom, I exhort you to wholeheartedly notice instances when you offer encouragement to others, as well as instances when you feel or receive encouragement from others. Pursuing the disposition of encouragement exposes a teacher's heart, uplifts their spirits, and champions the students and colleagues around them.

Pause and Reflect

1. When have you offered words of encouragement to your students and colleagues? What ripple effects have you seen or experienced?
2. Consider a time when you felt fully present in the classroom? How do you perceive your students feel in these moments?
3. Recall an instance when your students felt discouraged and then consider how your words and actions shifted this feeling for students?
4. Do you agree that encouragement can serve as a motivator for students? Why or why not?
5. Have you ever received encouragement that inspired you to become an encourager yourself? Reflect on the specific words or actions that moved you in this way.

References

AMLE (2021). *Tips for finishing the year strong: Advice and lessons learned from Association for Middle Level Education's Leadership Institute faculty.* https://www.amle.org/10-tips-for-finishing-the-year-strong-advice-and-lessons-learned-from-amles-leadership-institute-faculty/

Coleman, L. L., & Dotter, A. (2020). On the value of being in the moment in honors education. *Journal of the National Collegiate Honors Council, 21*(2), 19–24. http://digitalcommons.unl.edu/nchcjournal/655/

Dadandi, P. U., & Dadandi, I. (2022). The relationship among teachers' behaviours that encourage students' reading engagement, reading enjoyment, reading self-efficacy and reading success. *Participatory Educational Research, 9*(3), 98–110. https://doi.org/10.17275/per.22.56.9.3

Egbert, J. (2020). You are doing better than you think you are. *Association for Middle Level Education Magazine, 8*(4), 23–25. https://www.amle.org/youre-doing-better-than-you-think-you-are/

Glazer, S. (1999). *The heart of learning: Spirituality in education.* Tarcher Putnam.

Jensen, E. (2008). *Brain-based learning* (2nd ed.). Corwin Press.

Mackesy, C. (2019). *The boy, the mole, the fox and the horse.* Harper One.

Merriam-Webster (2023). Courage. *In Merriam-Webster.com Dictionary.* https://www.merriam-webster.com/dictionary/courage

Mielke, C. (2021). How cognitive distortions undermine well-being: Taking time to address our thinking traps is a form of self-care all educators can use. *Educational Leadership, 78*(4), 17–20. https://www.ascd.org/el/articles/how-cognitive-distortions-undermine-well-being

Minkel, J. (2020). In a time of calamity, what do children need from us? *Educational Leadership, 78*(3), 14–18. https://www.ascd.org/el/articles/in-a-time-of-calamity-what-do-children-need-from-us

Pendola, A., Marshall, D. T., Pressley, T., & Trammell, D. L. (2023). Why teachers leave: It isn't what you think. *Phi Delta Kappan, 105*(1), 51–55. https://doi.org/10.1177/00317217231197477

Richards, J. (2007). How effective principals encourage their teachers. *Principal, 86*(3), 48–50. https://www.naesp.org/sites/default/files/resources/2/Principal/2007/J-Fp48.pdf

Rowell, L., & Hong, E. (2013). Academic motivation: Concepts, strategies, and counseling approaches. *Professional School Counseling, 16*(3), 158–171.

Ryan, K., Cooper, J. M., & Bolick, C. M. (2016). *Those who can, teach.* Cengage Learning.

Simpson, S., & Millikan, M. (2023). *The power of hope: What we can learn about middle school from seventh grade inaugural poetry contest finalist Gabby Marshall.* AMLE. https://www.amle.org/the-power-of-hope-what-we-can-learn-about-middle-school-from-7th-grade-inaugural-poetry-contest-finalist-gabby-marshall/

Taulbert, C. L. (2006). *Eight habits of the heart for educators.* Corwin Press.

9

Inclusion

Introduction

I recently attended a forum with students and faculty at my college. The forum's purpose was to get people talking without debate—listening, responding, and hearing different viewpoints. Participants volunteered to discuss free speech: its role and its impact in higher education. The gathering was well organized with explicit norms and expectations shared at the start and students and faculty sat at round tables so they could share their opinions, questions, and experiences about free speech. My table discussed many topics, including representation, the need to belong, power imbalances, and how to feel comfortable in uncomfortable spaces. Students shared a desire to voice ideas and opinions without fear of judgment in order to promote healthy conversations and deliberation. Students also inquired about how to foster an environment of welcome where they might engage in uncomfortable conversations. For instance, when students discussed safety—both physical and emotional safety—participants discovered how inclusion can take the form of hospitality and shared belonging as well as how inclusion can look like concern and advocacy for marginalized groups. This opportunity for dialogue was a distinct reminder that inclusion can take many forms. I walked away from the deliberation with a sense of pride, in all the best ways, and was so impressed by the student participants who affirmed the faith I already had

DOI: 10.4324/9781003379539-9

in them. I was also reminded that today's students are agents of change; just as John Dewey anticipated, they are focused on serving well as productive citizens for the future (Ryan et al., 2015). I'll borrow the words of educator Carol Ann Tomlinson to reinforce this point: "My students are my best teachers" (2015, p. 90); students help us see the world through cultural and racial experiences that may not be like our own.

Links Between Hospitality and Inclusion

As I study dispositions, I have discovered that inclusion and hospitality are inextricably linked. Teachers practice both the physical hospitality of creating home-like classroom spaces and the intangible hospitality of cultivating a shared experience of welcome. Both forms of hospitality are foundational for inclusion: a teacher's attitude, body language, or voice can convey welcome and belonging and so can a classroom's walls that are adorned with student writings and artwork. We truly honor our students when we offer hospitality, in both explicit and subtle ways, as an expression of care and love. As teachers, we must routinely consider what actions and attitudes make students feel cared for.

Years ago, I wrote a short article that compared a classroom to a dinner party (Hughes, 2015). I have shared the dinner party analogy through the years and it has served as a point of reference as I work with student teachers. When my family hosts a dinner party in our home, we prepare, plan, organize, and cook. We welcome guests with enthusiasm, offer them a beverage or an appetizer, and invite them to sit down at a beautiful table. Ideally, there are lively exchanges, rich conversations, and the guests leave satisfied and filled with food and connection. I equate a dinner party and paying attention to the details, engaging in rich conversation, and inviting guests to return to how we invite students into learning in our classrooms. The dinner party analogy serves as a powerful reminder of welcome and purposeful preparation that validates those in attendance. Even on the non-ideal days when teachers may not feel eager to teach, we can still make the choice to offer this type of hospitality.

At the beginning of full-time student teaching placements, I see cooperating teachers demonstrate hospitality in a multitude of ways: they model gracious listening, field countless questions, engage in dialogue, offer constructive feedback, and share curriculum to support student teachers. In the same way, before the school year starts, at back-to-school nights and meet-the-teacher days, teachers ease student and parent anxiety with an introduction and initial welcome to the classroom. Hospitality like this creates a feeling for its recipients, yet it is more than a feeling. When demonstrated, hospitality can be conveyed with an open posture, welcoming words, or an inviting message. Hospitality can be a powerful disposition on its own; however, when we cultivate hospitality alongside inclusion, we can make the intangible merits of belonging and value more tangible for our students.

When I think of hospitality, I also think of service. I appreciate the way Thomas Hoerr crafts the distinction that, "Service is the technical delivery of a product. Hospitality is how the delivery of that product makes the recipient feel. Service is a monologue … hospitality, on the other hand, is a dialogue" (2014, pp. 91–92). It takes both service and hospitality to communicate belonging alongside an invitation to learn. David I. Smith's book, *Learning from the Stranger*, presents practices that infuse hospitality and service with practical suggestions to be attentive to others, strive to understand others, and learn from others (2009). Smith advocates for a particular form of hospitality that reaches across difference. When we engage as humans, across diverse cultures, ethnicities, languages, races, regions, and spiritually through inclusion and hospitality, we can learn and grow together.

Hospitality should be viewed not as a single set of specific tasks or actions, but as a structure for responsively meeting students' and parents' needs (Latunde, 2019). Parents, like students, thrive when they feel included in a school community; the traditional invitations to school events are important, but going beyond to see and value parents as assets who enrich the school community affirms them in unique and empowering ways. In my local community, I have observed school principals send vans to pick up parents who don't have reliable transportation for evening meetings at schools. I have also witnessed principals invite parents to cook and share food from their cultures before a school open house. Additionally, I see an increasing number of schools offer translation services to bilingual and multilingual families so that parents can access important school information in their home language. Prioritizing access for students and parents conveys genuine hospitality and demonstrates a school's investment in and commitment to equitable resources and inclusion.

Inclusion or Exclusion?

It is not a surprise to the readers of this book that educators expend a lot of energy on students. Teachers actively work to decipher who students are, what they need, and where their learning gaps are in order to welcome them into learning. As we dive deeper into understanding how to demonstrate inclusion, I recommend taking time to reflect on your own experiences of inclusion *and* your own experiences of exclusion. When we are invited to a social gathering, we may feel included or we may feel we have access to a group or an opportunity. In contrast, when we hear about a social gathering to which we are not included, we may feel excluded or feel that the group is being exclusive. There are far more complex examples of inclusion or exclusion, yet it is critical to acknowledge how our own feelings and experiences impact how we convey, respond to, and demonstrate inclusion.

One assignment in my introductory education course prompts students to articulate in writing how they want to be known as a professional. Students write about how, in their first teaching positions, they may be asked to serve on a committee at their school. I ask students to brainstorm how they will listen, use their voices, respond to others, and disagree. After completing the brainstorming, students participate in mock committees with a decision-making task. They are then asked to wrestle with a variety of talking points or hot-button educational issues. For instance, one of the tasks focuses on discussing the value of and need for homework. Another task involves decision-making about funding for extracurricular programs such as sports or visual and performing arts. After students participate in the mock committee meetings, we debrief together. Students reflect on their role on the committee, how they used their voices, how they presented their opinions, and how they listened to others. During these discussions, I appreciate students' unique perspectives, such as "I learned that I am able to listen well to others, but I need to fully formulate my thoughts before speaking" or "I like leading discussions and contributing." Other responses include, "I learned that I am quick to make assumptions" or "Something I learned about myself is that it is important for me to collect my thoughts before I speak." I find that this mock committee exercise builds greater self-awareness as students consider their thoughts, actions, and responses to others. Some students realize that they need to develop greater capacity for problem solving and using their professional voices at times, while other students internalize the importance of listening to counter-voices with sensitivity and a posture of openness. Thus, pre-service programs and pre-service faculty can help teacher candidates first identify and examine their preconceptions and then move toward new or expanded perspectives and understandings.

Circling back to Chapter 1 and the idea of humanizing the dispositions valued in teaching, I came across a study that highlights behavioral indicators that include teacher beliefs and understandings. Of significance, the indicator of a teacher's commitment to teach all students stands out; for example, maintaining high expectations for all students regardless of their progress and abilities conveys a palpable commitment to growing one's cultural sensitivity and moral compass (Feiman-Nemser & Schussler, 2010, pp. 181–182). As teachers face increasing challenges related to students' mental health, the LGBTQ+ community, social media distractions, bullying, and the pursuit of racial equity and reconciliation in schools, we must foster dispositions that underscore the common humanity in our students, our staffs, and ourselves. As teachers strive to stand in the gap for students, carving out time and opportunities to reflect, discuss, and collaborate, as well as examine assumptions and personal backgrounds, become essential for developing and demonstrating inclusion (Feiman-Nemser & Schussler, 2010, p. 187). When teachers teach, they make a conscious choice to care deeply about the students in front of them and the education they provide for them (Tomlinson, 2015). Educator Paige Ray asserts that students are instruments of change where their authority and dignity are affirmed through invitation, trust, and boundaries in *community*. Moreover, upholding a student's individual dignity promotes the dignity of the whole classroom and larger school community (2022).

Notably, a school-wide culture of inclusion begins with school leaders and teachers. All employees in a school community can add value to students' lives (McCormick, 2022). A school's classified staff has a critical role to play in school climate and operations; school groundskeepers, cafeteria workers, painters, electricians, administrative assistants, bus drivers, and custodial staff are part of a school community and its ethos. Inclusion means showing respect for every member of the school community. Just like with our students, teachers and school leaders can get to know staff members and their interests, share clear communications with the community, invite classified staff to serve on committees, and work hand in hand with certified staff (McCormick, 2022). Intentional action steps can also include meeting with staff one-on-one, sharing school communications with all employees, inviting employees repeatedly to school meetings and events, asking classified staff what they need, enlisting their problem-solving skills, and showing them appreciation. These suggestions remind me of my high school administrator days when I realized the benefit of taking time to get to know my custodial staff with check-ins and acts of appreciation; recognizing that the inclusion of all staff members affects students is the first step to growing a positive school climate. Building an inclusive community means all constituents look out for each other.

Educators need to create space for students to feel physically and emotionally safe—principals and districts need to do the same for teachers. Student learning soars when students feel safe and supported by their teacher. Because universal education values all students, teachers serve all students that enter their classrooms (Kanold, 2021; Ryan et al., 2015). Schools must strive to cultivate communities that encourage uplifting exchanges between teachers and students as well as between students and their peers. Parker Palmer framed this idea beautifully; "Community knows how to welcome the soul and help us hear its voice ..." (Palmer, 2004, p 22).

Even though we have already explored the disposition of reflection in Chapter 3, it is important to point out that providing time and space to cultivate a school's reflective climate results in increased trust and openness. Educator Michelle Hope notes that humans find strength when they are valued, heard, and understood (2022, p. 50). To build a network of support for teachers, she suggests addressing teachers' human and emotional needs before the academic ones. In addition, psychological ownership for teachers (and others in a school community) grows from within and involves both cognitive and emotional elements that create a sense of belonging, or a sense of being at home in the school community (Feirsen, 2022). Feeling a sense of belonging, connection, and safety all play a role in inclusion; when there is a sense of psychological ownership among teachers and school constituents, an inclusive culture can develop.

Culturally Responsiveness

Inclusion, as defined by educational consultant Lauren Porosoff, is the assimilation of those that have been marginalized (2022). Porosoff asks if the marginalized are represented in authentic ways. She concludes that if learners see their own experiences and those that are different from them in classroom curricula, they are more likely to think carefully about the experiences of others. Thus, it is critical for teachers to have a real voice in selecting classroom materials and content that is culturally relevant as well as supports and represents diverse learners (National Association of Elementary School Principals, 2023).

In recent years, global issues such as immigration and racial reconciliation have taken center stage and led to the end goal of helping students and teachers feel that they are on the same team and part of a larger group or community (Hoerr, 2016). At the same time, there has been some pushback among educators who question an increased educational focus on equity or diversity. For instance, some educators question why previous equity initiatives have been unsuccessful. Principal Gina Davenport notes that sometimes educators don't understand a school's equity goals or schools may not have a shared vocabulary for equity. In these instances, Davenport suggests getting on a figurative "balcony" to change perspective. By going to a balcony to gain perspective, educators can assess what is really happening and what is needed in their schools (2022). In 2020, during the height of the pandemic when there was a stream of political unrest in the United States, I realized that I needed to go to this type of balcony to address my own biases and assumptions. Taking time to reflect and gain new perspective delivered a dose of humility to me. For instance, I realized that there are times that I need to directly address a class of students or individual students, reframe a question to a student, and name my privilege and biases. Sometimes, I need to lean in and listen to my students' stories and ask better questions. Last year, for example, I distinctly recall showing a video clip to one of my classes. While my class and I watched the video clip, I caught my breath and stopped the video. In the moment, I realized that the video didn't include any students or teachers of color and I humbly addressed my class to let them know that the video was not an authentic representation of the future K-12 students they would teach. Looking back on this experience, I felt embarrassed, convicted, and vulnerable, while at the same time, I felt grateful (and still do) for opportunities to authentically address assumptions and biases in my own teaching, most especially because my actions and choices impact my students and their perspectives on education and inclusion long after they have been students in my classroom.

How schools and educators respond to issues of equity, inequity, and marginalization matters (Davenport, 2022). It is important to acknowledge that a diverse faculty and a diverse student body simply "getting along" doesn't equate to equity.

Understanding this, Principal Gina Davenport advocates for a focus on school equity to problem solve and protect diverse voices. A team of authors extends Davenport's thinking, noting that school initiatives for improvement are traditionally about organizational structure and steps. If school leaders place emphasis on the humans involved, on building a culture of trust, the effort pays dividends for the school community (Mehta et al., 2022). Additionally, an inclusive school culture has a shared vision that seeks to remove barriers for individuals and the larger system. School leaders must make efforts to ensure that inclusive school environments are supported with cultural and equitable instructional practices that honor all constituents (Houck & Corcoran, 2022).

Decades ago, culturally responsive teaching was introduced in an effort to promote linking cultural content to students' backgrounds. Authentically examining and understanding students requires teaching and pedagogy that engages students across cultures and disciplines. Culturally responsive teaching necessitates a holistic approach that honors student motivation alongside culture, emphasizing that a student's response to learning activities may vary based upon their culture and experiences (Wlodkowski & Ginsberg, 1995). In addition, culturally responsive teaching also expects that teachers *and* all school employees are culturally competent so they can provide a rigorous and high-quality education, as well as hold high expectations to empower students (Gonzales, 2023). School communities can seek to specifically understand and increase students' intrinsic motivation for learning when they establish conditions of inclusion and develop attitudes to embrace learning. Also, defining learning tasks that genuinely honor students' backgrounds further connects students to course content for optimal learning.

Working with others, we recognize the role of culture and its influence on ourselves as well as on others (Luckner & Rudolph, 2009). By doing so, we increase our own awareness and capacity to understand other individuals. Taking time to learn about our own personal cultures, our attitudes, behaviors, and biases related to diversity, and reflecting on our own knowledge and beliefs informs our teaching and celebrates difference. Practical suggestions to increase our own cultural capacity can include sharing a meal with students or colleagues, or discussing the needs, similarities, and differences among cultures, or expressing belief in students' ability to learn and respect others (p. 60). Moreover, recent research asserts that in order to build students' social-emotional skills in schools, school curriculum must recognize the cultural, racial, and ethnic backgrounds of students. Social and emotional learning, discussed in the preface of this book, focuses on the needs of each child, *the whole child*, and teaching SEL contributes to the healthy development of children. When a school focuses on SEL, it provides an inviting foundation for inclusion and student flourishing to develop student agency, recognize student assets, foster connects, prioritize individuals, as well as support a school staff's social and emotional needs (Kubatzky, 2023).

Currently, there is increased attention around the complicated issue of grading practices. Although it is not surprising that grading is a complex subject, educators do their best to create rubrics, establish norms, and be objective with grading. A teacher's assumptions, contexts, student behaviors, and environments play a part in grading outcomes, that, in full transparency, are not always objective. In a time when grading practices and priorities vary from department to department, school to school, and district to district, Joe Feldman addresses equitable grading practices and implementation in his book, *Grading for Equity* (2019). In an effort to encourage teachers to value knowledge, cultivate a growth mindset, and resist bias, Feldman presents research on equity, motivation, educational psychology, and teaching and learning that influences grading. He challenges the status quo with a focus on accuracy, bias resistance, and motivation so to support students and promote their academic success (p. 227–228).

An additional angle to consider as we explore nurturing attitudes and postures of inclusion pertains to learning differences. Schools are expected to serve and provide "students with disabilities access and opportunities in general education classrooms in ways that are similar to their nondisabled peers, utilizing accommodations and modifications needed to succeed" (Adams & Ostovar, 2023, p. 33). Research estimates that while approximately 6.7 million American children currently have Individualized Education Plans (IEPs), the numbers are expected to increase in future years. Hence, finding additional strategies, methods, and funding to support *all* students through enriching programs, services, instructional support, and appropriate staffing becomes increasingly essential for school inclusion (Franks, 2023).

Ownership, Assets, and Voice

In a recent class discussion on inclusion, one of my undergraduates defined inclusion as "honoring everyone." To honor a person means "to regard or treat (someone) with admiration and respect" (Merriam-Webster, 2023). Honoring every student translates to seeing each student, each person, as an individual. Recognizing students' assets puts a focus on students' strengths rather than on their limitations. In contrast, deficit thinking assumes that students from marginalized backgrounds struggle in school because of their circumstances. Researcher and psychologist Kelsie Reed defines deficit thinking as blaming the victim. She also views deficit thinking as a social justice issue; marginalized students, students of color, students with learning differences, and students from lower socioeconomic backgrounds are impacted the most (2020). A similar no excuses approach suggests that educators ask themselves, "What are we not doing for this student, or what does this student need in order to be successful?" Deficit thinking most often involves blaming a student, their parents, or their culture for a student's lack of progress at school. This approach can be detrimental because, in these instances, teachers can give up on students or lower their expectations for students (Reed, 2020). In contrast, an assets-based approach to students translates to honoring, seeing, and valuing individual students for what they bring to the classroom. Teachers extend and affirm students' value by recognizing and celebrating their assets and strengths (Wortman, 2012).

In my first teaching position years ago, I recall a professional development day where my principal secured a bus for the school's teachers. The bus drove our principal and team of teachers through our community's neighborhoods with the purpose of physically seeing where our junior high students lived. The bus ride presented a tangible picture of students' diverse home lives and living conditions. As we drove by dense apartment complexes, suburban neighborhoods with sprawling homes, and homeless camps, teachers felt the impact. When we debriefed with our principal, we recognized a shift in our teacher perspectives; the exercise prompted us to look beyond the test scores and behaviors of our students to truly see and know our students and their stories. The experience was humbling and pushed our team of teachers, including me, out of our comfort zone; we were forced to look beyond our limited perspectives to understand students' backgrounds and circumstances.

Exploring barriers that students may be facing can be an additional approach to understanding inclusion (Fisher & Frey, 2021). Instead of making assumptions about students with thoughts such as "they don't get it, they don't care, or they are checked out," teachers can resist focusing on students' outward behaviors. As an alternative, teachers can consider the root causes of student behavior. As referred to earlier in *Dispositions Are a Teacher's Greatest Strength*, learning about our students and what they carry in their backpacks (Hughes, 2014) serves to inform how we respond to students and ultimately how we teach them. Engaging in conversations with students about their interests (what they find fun or interesting in school), or even asking them how they like to learn, communicates teacher care and intentionality that can nurture student confidence. Finding avenues to connect with students in ways that are important to them can lead to meaningful relationships that can make a difference (Betz, 2021).

Promoting higher-level discussions and developing student voices, especially those that might be marginalized, gives students skills and access to the larger conversation. Building on student's pre-existing critical thinking assets through discussion and collaborative assignments can also boost students' academic success and self-advocacy skills (Parker, 2023). All students need opportunities to engage, and they have meaningful contributions to share. Cultivating student voice further honors students' stories, connections, and confidence. Teacher efforts to talk less, value students' questions over their answers, and make reflection part of classroom routines, are additional methods that convey inclusion and honor students' differences. These approaches make room for student voices and critical thinking, allowing both students and teachers to foster knowledge and grow together (Safir, 2023); giving students greater ownership and opportunity in learning spaces elevates their voices and values their contributions.

The Heart and Practice of Inclusion

For career sustainability, educators must experience and re-experience community, collaboration, a love of learning, as well as a sense of purpose, vision, and belonging in their work. Reminding teachers of their purpose, *their why*, reinforces their initial decision to teach and reminds them of their purpose. When considering how to implement inclusive teaching practices, I've learned how necessary and how challenging inclusion can be. When schools make inclusion integral to their mission and values, inclusion becomes a community responsibility. Superintendents, principals, deans, and teachers must make efforts to move forward *and* as we do, we must look at ourselves. I appreciate Christopher Day's perspective that seems to captures the heart and soul of inclusion for teachers: "Passionate teachers are aware of the challenge of the broader social contexts in which they teach, have a clear sense of identity, and believe that they can make a difference to the learning and achievement of all their pupils" (2004, p. 2). When educators work with others that are different from us, we recognize the role of culture and its influence on ourselves as well as its influences on others; additionally, when we do, we actually increase our self-awareness and capacity to understand others (Luckner & Rudolph, 2009). Taking time to learn about our own cultures, alongside learning about the cultures of others (for example our diverse attitudes, behaviors, and biases), as well as taking time to reflect on our own knowledge and beliefs informs how we teach and interact with our students and colleagues. Increasing our individual and collective cultural capacity whether sharing a meal with students, discussing their needs, recognizing similarities and differences among cultures, or believing that all students can learn conveys and uplifts the unique gifts that educators have to offer (p. 60). Together, we can commit to developing postures of inclusion that translate to learning from others, caring for others, and honoring others. This is the only *why* we need.

Pause and Reflect

1. Did Chapter 9 frame inclusion for you in new ways?
2. How might inclusion's links to hospitality and service shape your responses to students, parents, and colleagues?
3. What barriers to inclusion do you face in your school community and classroom?
4. Identify several strategies that you can explore to promote and convey openness, access, welcome, and belonging in your classroom?
5. Which dispositions explored in *Dispositions Are a Teacher's Greatest Strength* point you to the disposition of inclusion?

References

Adams, K., & Ostovar, S. (2023). Words of inclusion. *Principal, 102*(3), 33. https://www.naesp.org/resource/words-of-inclusion/

Betz, A. (2021). Using youtube to reach, teach, and differentiate. *Association for Middle Level Educators*.https://www.amle.org/using-youtube-to-reach-teach-and-differentiate/

Davenport, G. (2022). Adaptive leadership for school equity. *Educational Leadership, 79*(6), 20–29. https://www.ascd.org/el/articles/adaptive-leadership-for-school-equity

Day, C. (2004). *A passion for teaching*. Routledge.

Feiman-Nemser, & Schussler (2010). Defining, developing, and assessing dispositions, a cross-case analysis. In P. C. Murrel, M. Diez, S. Feiman-Nemser, & D. L. Schussler (Eds.), *Teaching as a moral practice: Defining, developing, and assessing professional dispositions in teacher education* (pp. 177–202). Harvard Education Press.

Feirsen, R. (2022). Why teacher buy-in is overrated. *Educational Leadership, 79*(6), 49–52. https://www.ascd.org/el/articles/why-teacher-buy-in-is-overrated

Feldman, J. (2019). *Grading for equity. What it is, why it matters, and how it can transform schools and classrooms*. Corwin.

Fisher, D., & Frey, N. (2021). Show and tell: A video column/Why do students disengage? *Educational Leadership, 79*(1), 76–77. https://www.ascd.org/el/articles/show-and-tell-a-video-column-why-do-students-disengage

Franks, L. E. (2023). Closing gaps for students with disabilities. *Principal, 102*(3), 60. https://www.naesp.org/resource/closing-gaps-for-students-with-disabilities/

Gonzales, M. (2023). Is your curriculum culturally responsive? *Principal, 102*(4),31–34.https://www.naesp.org/resource/is-your-curriculum-culturally-responsive/

Hoerr, T. R. (2014). Service vs. hospitality. *Educational Leadership, 71*(6), 91–92. https://www.ascd.org/el/articles/service-vs.-hospitality

Hoerr, T. R. (2016). Protecting your team. *Educational Leadership, 74*(3), 89–90. https://www.ascd.org/el/articles/protecting-your-team

Hope, M. (2022). Prioritizing connection. *Educational Leadership, 80*(2), 50–55. https://www.ascd.org/el/articles/prioritizing-connection

Houck, B. D., & Corcoran, T. F. (2022). Prioritize to stabilize. *Principal, 102*(1), 46–48. https://www.naesp.org/resource/prioritize-to-stabilize/

Hughes, M. C. (2014). What's in your backpack? *Association for Middle Level Education Magazine, 1*(9), 19.

Hughes, M. C. (2015). The classroom and the dinner party. *Association for Middle Level Education Magazine, 2*(5), 24–25.

Kanold, T. D. (2021). *Soul! fulfilling the promise of your professional life.* Solution Tree Press.

Kubatzky, L. (2023). Inclusive SEL helps students thrive. *Principal, 102*(3). https://www.naesp.org/resource/inclusive-sel-helps-students-thrive/

Latunde, Y. (2019). Towards more inclusive schools: An application of hospitality in parental involvement. *International Christian Community of Teacher Educators Journal, 14*(2). https://digitalcommons.georgefox.edu/cgi/viewcontent.cgi?article=1143&context=icctej

Luckner, J., & Rudolph, S. (2009). *Teach well, live well.* Corwin.

McCormick, M. D. (2022). Key contributors to school climate. *Principal, 102*(1), 38–40. https://www.naesp.org/resource/key-contributors-to-school-climate/

Mehta, J., Yurkofsky, M., & Frumin, K. (2022). Linking continuous improvement and adaptive leadership. *Educational Leadership, 79*(6), 36–41. https://www.ascd.org/el/articles/linking-continuous-improvement-and-adaptive-leadership

Merriam-Webster (2023). Honor. In *Merriam-Webster.com Dictionary.* https://www.merriam-webster.com/dictionary/honor

National Association of Elementary School Principals (2023). Teachers want more aligned materials. *Principal, 102*(3), 12. https://naesp.ygsclicbook.com/pubs/principal/2023/janfeb-2023/live/index.html#p=15

Palmer, P. (2004). *A hidden wholeness: The journey toward an undivided life.* Jossey-Bass.

Parker, K. N. (2023). Black kids have something to say–if we listen. *Educational Leadership, 80*(7), 74–75. https://www.ascd.org/el/articles/black-kids-have-something-to-say-if-we-listen

Porosoff, L. (2022). Which curriculum audit is best for your school? *Educational Leadership, 79*(5), 66–67. https://www.ascd.org/el/articles/which-curriculum-audit-is-best-for-your-school

Ray, P. (2022). On authority and dignity. In K. Badley, & M. Patrick (Eds.), *The complexities of authority in the classroom* (pp. 132–140). Routledge Taylor & Francis Group. https://doi.org/10.4324/9781003140849

Reed, K. (2020). Deficit thinking in schools is a social justice issue. Here's why we need do better. *Lessons for SEL.* https://www.10publications.com/blog/deficit-thinking-in-schools-a-social-justice-issue

Ryan, K., Cooper, J. M., & Bolick, C. M. (2015). *Those who can teach, teach* (14th ed.). Cengage.

Safir, S. (2023). Cultivating a pedagogy of student voice. *Educational Leadership, 80*(7), 50–53. https://www.ascd.org/el/articles/cultivating-a-pedagogy-of-student-voice

Smith, D. I. (2009). *Learning from the stranger.* Wm. B. Eerdmans Publishing Company.

Tomlinson, C. A. (2015). One to grow on/the caring teacher's manifesto. *Educational Leadership, 72*(6), 89–90. https://www.ascd.org/el/articles/the-caring-teachers-manifesto

Tomlinson, C. A. (2015). Being human in the classroom. *Education Leadership, 73*(2), 74–77. https://www.ascd.org/el/articles/being-human-in-the-classroom

Wlodkowski, R. J., & Ginsberg, M. B. (1995). A framework for culturally responsive teaching. *Educational Leadership, 53*(1). https://www.ascd.org/el/articles/a-framework-for-culturally-responsive-teaching

Wortman, S. (2012). *Hospitality.* In A. L. Dee, & G. Tiffin (Eds.), *Faithful education* (pp. 62–76). Pickwick Publications.

10

Collaboration

The Importance of Collaboration

The teaching profession at its best possesses partnerships between colleagues and their educational communities that elevate curriculum, build relationships, and serve students well. Teaching necessitates collaboration—teamwork between teachers and students, colleagues and colleagues, teachers and parents, parents and students, teachers and administrators, and administrators and parents. As with the other dispositions in this book, possessing and developing a collaborative skillset comes easier to some teachers than others. Working and cooperating with colleagues can look very different depending on the task, school community, and school leadership team.

Fostering collaborative skills takes effort and intentionality. I taught junior high school the first seven years of my educational career. During this time, I experienced the coming and going of four principals. In the years that followed, when I served as a high school administrator, my district cycled through a collection of superintendents, principals, and assistant principals. Some of these leaders possessed amazing skills that empowered, unified, and moved the school community forward. Other leaders lacked a clear vision or struggled to build a school team. These contrasting experiences reveal that collaboration can be challenging and may or may not be prioritized or modeled by school leadership.

DOI: 10.4324/9781003379539-10

Interestingly, collaboration can often be the missing link in school reform (Jones, 2021; Leana, 2011). Suggestions to foster collaboration include nurturing relationships, making space for collaboration, and sharing tasks and responsibilities. The most successful collaborations actually occur when teachers share burdens and learn from one another (Jones, 2021). When teachers collaborate, they see the perspectives and priorities of others, and they are better able to enlarge and even revise their approaches to teaching. Partnering with other teachers and learning from each other taps into both human and social capital (Leana, 2011). Human capital recognizes a teacher's experience, knowledge, and skills collectively. In contrast, the concept of social capital values the relationships among teachers: building a colleague's confidence, experience, opinions, and professional wisdom increases social capital. Human and social capital are mutually affirming for teachers; investing in both is worth the time and effort.

As mentioned in Chapter 5 on adaptability, teachers make hundreds of decisions every day, whether working alone in their classrooms or meeting in teams to analyze and develop curricula. It is not surprising that teachers, by nature, regularly engage with others: students, parents, administrators, and colleagues. Curiously, in the last decade, the rise of professional learning communities, or PLCs, has pushed teachers to collaborate and work together toward common goals and decisions about curriculum and school policies. As a result, teachers need to be increasingly ready to ask thoughtful, clarifying questions, use I statements, and listen well to engage in productive dialogue. Even when these conditions are met, navigating conflicts and misunderstandings remain part of the job (Levin & Schrum, 2017). Teachers are expected to actively listen to address conflict, use their professional voices, and respond to others; intentionally striving to nurture skills for collaborative-rich environments benefits teachers, students, and the larger school community.

Sharon Feiman-Nemser and Deborah Schussler's research (2010) recognizes that collaborative skills are essential skills in teacher training, most especially, because embracing collaboration can result in greater teacher effectiveness. In recent years,

learning to lean into the disposition of collaboration—to participate in collegial interactions with a spirit of inquiry, openness,
and curiosity—has become more important in educational
circles. Unlike in years past when teachers were left to make curricular decisions on their own, more recently, PLCs have become
an increasingly integral part of teaching. Just like players in
team sports, basketball and hockey for instance, teachers serve
on grade-level teams and on PLCs that rely on participation to
elevate and better the team. Just as my son's high school basketball coach expects his players to make those around them, those
on the team, better, today's teachers are expected to be team
players who possess a willingness to collaborate on a wealth of
topics such as assessment data and practices, curriculum, mental
health supports, and more. This collaborative team approach
serves to honor and uplift others and stands in contrast to societal messages that espouse individualism over collaboration.

Years ago, leadership expert Robert Greenleaf created a theoretical framework for servant leadership that argues for vulnerability, making mistakes, and possessing a growth mindset
as essential components to servant leadership that uniquely
requires leaders to put others before themselves (Northouse,
2021). This leadership framework necessitates a high level of trust
(Hurt, 2021, p. 10). J. Ibeh Agvanyim's book, *The Five Principles
of Collaboration*, builds on this framework and proposes five
characteristics that collaborators need trust, respect, willingness,
empowerment, and effective communication. Agvanyim believes
that individuals who engage in collaboration recognize the
responsibility of being a role model to others even when others
are not looking (2015). Fostering positive relationships with
others remains foundational to our work as educators. Whether
we are working with colleagues, administrators, students, or
parents, we need to develop skills and dispositions that nurture
positive relationships; communicating well, building rapport,
listening with empathy, and displaying curiosity are all pathways
for developing the relational capacity that teachers need. Thus,
district and school leadership should note that thoughtfully
organized professional development time can make room for collaborative conversations and skill building so educators can work

together to resolve conflicts and be agents of change (Luckner & Rudolph, 2009).

Collaboration in Action

Long gone are the days of siloed teaching and planning by yourself. I remember when I first started teaching junior high English in the late 1980s—my principal handed me a textbook full of short stories and a pamphlet with the four types of writing I needed to teach. Although there wasn't a clear roadmap, or pacing guide, or even standards to guide me through my first days on the job, I appreciated the creativity and freedom I was given with the meager materials. In retrospect, I've noticed years later that today's principals, schools, and districts are doing a better job setting up new teachers for success with collaborative PLCs. Collaborative skills are essential as teachers design curriculum and assessments together, analyze data, and discuss student progress in collaborative teams. We often hear the statement, "There is no I in the word team" which translates to collaboration moving us from working alone to working with others. Developing effective school leaders who can create conditions for collaboration are needed more than ever before. Having a shared vision for decision-making focused on what is best for those involved and what is specifically best for students serves to further elevate teacher collaboration. Unfortunately, school growth can be stunted when we focus solely on our own individual needs and perspectives (Murphy, 2022), but creating team spirit or finding the "we" in team fosters collaboration for potential growth.

My graduate school had a public relations campaign with the message, "Be Known." This messaging has stuck with me through the years so much so that when I reflect on my work with colleagues and students, I frequently ask them, "How do you want to be known?" Asking my undergraduate students to pause and reflect about how they teach and interact with students and colleagues remains a fundamental question I want them to respond to. This question encourages me, and those to whom I pose it, to contemplate how we can offer support, participate, and collaborate with others. Through the years, I have thoroughly enjoyed seeing student teachers thrive when they engage with grade-level teams and PLCs during full-time student teaching. A PLC typically serves as a setting where student teachers' thinking and assumptions are challenged. They experience firsthand how to use their professional voices. Knowing they are not alone and are with like-minded colleagues gives student teachers a boost. Equipping student teachers to use their voices, become problem solvers, and embrace learning from and with their colleagues (and students) strengthens their professionalism.

Paying attention to dispositions like collaboration can exercise and develop a teacher's cooperative skills. Giving novice and experienced teachers time to reflect on dispositions they see as professional assets, as well as those they need to strengthen, builds self-awareness (Levin & Schrum, p. 39). Helping student teachers identify what barriers or assumptions get in their way when they collaborate is critical as they develop professionally. Engaging in reflection and discussion around students' perceptions of themselves as well as their perceptions of others can build increased self-awareness and confidence for collaboration. Furthermore, becoming self-aware can grow an individual's emotional skills as well as entice others into working with them (Aruda, 2023). When collaboration is modeled by teachers, the skills become transferable to students and colleagues; collaboration also leads to improved academic outcomes for students (Fleming & Foster, 2022). For instance, teachers can use collaborative group work to encourage teamwork among students (Association for Middle Level Education, 2023). When grouping students, teachers can thoughtfully consider each assignment and the makeup for each group based on ability, diversity, demeanor, or even gender. What's more, collaborative opportunities support and grow communication, trust, integrity and responsibility among students. Educator and author Berit Gordon suggests creating flexible classrooms spaces for students to create and collaborate. When students collaborate, they become increasingly aware of their own values as well as whether or not they are inspiring, motivating, or empowering others (2020).

Collaboration's Benefits and Challenges

Keeping students at the center of our work as teachers remains a professional priority. By the same token, educators must consider how we respond and engage with our colleagues. Do we listen well? Do we hear others? Do we think before we speak? How do we deal with disagreement? Do we get angry? Do we listen to varying perspectives or do we make quick judgments and need to get our own way? Possessing a collaborative attitude and mindset necessitates asking questions like these. Ten chapters into *Dispositions Are a Teacher's Greatest Strength*, we know that dispositions, such as collaboration, require a measure of teacher self-awareness and intentionality. Today's pop culture created the term *collab*, which translates to collaboration or union between two musicians or two businesses for example. We see and hear about fashion collabs between clothing designers and musicians or between reality stars and professional athletes. Collabs such as these are not only lucrative for business and marketing, they create new interest in a product or brand. Of late, we see educational collaborations between colleagues, grade-level teams, discipline specific teams, and administrators. Nurturing a collaborative community conveys that we care for colleagues, cooperate, belong, and engage in a shared culture and vision. Regardless, even with the purest intentions, we must recognize that collaboration can be challenging. Whether serving on a school committee, partnering with parent associations, or engaging with a colleague, teachers must consider their influence and position as collaborators. A team of Harvard lecturers suggests that "Educators must first be learners who are open and willing to change their own hearts and minds. By doing so, they will be better able to create the conditions for others to learn and change as well" (Cheatham et al., 2023); bringing in and respecting others' voices can inspire new ideas and thinking. Notably, when teacher leaders feel that their voices are valued and heard, they are more likely to remain in the profession (Levin & Schrum, 2017, p. 7).

When educators strive to foster habits and structures for collaboration, reward comes their way. Trusting and putting our colleagues and students before ourselves can strengthen collaboration in community. Collaboration excels when an educator "seeks out collegial interactions to grow as a professional, enhance practice, and support students' learning. This includes modeling and promoting collaboration within his or her classroom" (Wenzel & Roberts, 2014, p. 1). In my experience, when I take the time to listen to a colleague's perspective on an issue, such as a proposed curricular change, I learn a lot. Sometimes, my colleague's added perspective changes my mind. Asking colleagues to weigh in on our classroom practices and routines can instill new ideas and suggestions for seating arrangements, discussion corners, and cooperative teams. Author David Brooks characterizes this essential skill as listening loudly (2023).

Early in my career, when I was a new junior high teacher and department chair, I hosted regular department meetings at my house and asked department colleagues to bring lessons and ideas to share. For the most part this was a successful and encouraging practice, because as a department, we found common ground as we shared assignments, swapped stories, and learned from each other. Reflecting decades later, I realize that even with the best intentions and well-planned opportunities for us to share ideas, I wasn't a skilled active listener. As a novice teacher, I lacked the ability and self-awareness to actively listen and affirm each member of my department for their contributions. Recalling an instance where I didn't listen well resulted in a scheduling conflict for the department. Had I spent more time listening to all members of the department, rather than just a few of the louder voices, I might have avoided sleepless nights and hard feelings over a decision I made. Chewing on the experience years later, my self-awareness and collaborative skills to listen and lean in to hear others' voices and opinions have grown. I find that even if the outcome doesn't match a particular colleague's expectation, the sincere effort to value and recognize others' opinions and vision becomes an essential part of professional practice that requires increased patience, reflection, and intention. Looking in the rearview mirror, I can attest that collaborating with colleagues improves my work and ultimately strengthens what I offer to my students. Engaging in informal and formal collaboration, whether through a brief exchange with a colleague in the hallway or more formally in a committee meeting, actually energizes me, makes me think, and enlarges my lens. I truly appreciate when my colleagues and I work alongside each other, challenge each other, and use our professional positions for good.

A collaborative-rich environment illuminates engaging in collective learning around shared interests, values, and goals for school improvement (Little, 2022). Sharing stories with colleagues and talking about emotions are proven strategies that promote a collaborative mindset (Aguilar, 2018, pp. 201–202). In addition, as discussed in Chapter 4, recognizing the importance of providing opportunities for colleagues to convey a sense of empathy to and for each other connects them (Knight, 2021). We shouldn't be surprised that teachers strive to equip students with skills and knowledge for life, so as lifelong learners ourselves, we can choose to strengthen our professional practice as community members who are eager to engage in collaborative practice.

Ian Murphy, editor of *Principal Magazine*, recognizes that educators value collaboration and a strong collaborative team spirit for school success (2022). I agree, but in reality, we know that collaborative teams can be challenging to organize, gather, and implement. To foster team spirit, teachers need to be open to learning from one another, disagreeing with one another, and listening to one another (Johnston et. al, 2009). Striving to celebrate and support teachers with a positive attitude can make a genuine difference. Demonstrating care, establishing communication, building trust, and nurturing confidence adds to an educator's personal strengths as well as the development of a shared vision (McCormick, 2022). School leader Jay Mathisen frames building school culture as "community with a cause"; this translates to recognizing the value of being part of team that enjoys being together. This type of unified engagement most often produces the reward of a strengthened community that is bonded, maintains a sense of belonging, and feels human (2022, p. 86). Likewise, a school community that possesses a spirit for communal improvement increases its collective agency, values teachers' voices, and makes decisions that are in the best interests of students (p. 87). Many school communities have a desire to strengthen the skills, knowledge, behaviors, and learning gaps resulting from the pandemic in order to serve students well (Fleming & Foster, 2022); in response, educators shouldn't ignore the power of harnessing buy-in and ownership from within their school community. Being part of a collaborative community with a shared vision and desire to solve problems can energize teachers, administrators, parents, and students toward common goals.

Extended Collaboration

As educators prepare students for the democratic citizenship that John Dewey envisioned in the late 1800s and early 1900s, schools can consider strengthening collaborative ties with parents to uplift both the school community and student achievement. I keenly recall organizing a fieldtrip fundraiser when I first started teaching junior high school where I orchestrated a night for students and families to raise money for busses and tickets to see the renowned play, *Phantom of the Opera*, in Los Angeles. Orchestrating a large fundraiser by myself felt daunting so, at the urging of my principal, I reached out to my students' parents for help. The invitation to parents was well received, resulting in parents partnering on the fundraiser's food, student presentations, fundraiser set-up and clean-up. Parents were willing and so capable; they went the extra mile to help bring the fundraiser and fieldtrip to fruition. Most importantly, as a new teacher, I discovered the value of involving and collaborating with parents as partners. Now, years later, when I run into former students and parents in my community, they remind me that the fundraiser and fieldtrip were highlights from their junior high school years; the experience introduced me and my students to the value of collaboration and developing skills of collaboration within our school community.

Undoubtedly, teachers know that collaborating with parents isn't always smooth, but choosing to partner together to do what's best for students can reap reward for all involved. Until I had children of my own, I did not fully grasp how deeply parents want what's best for their children—and they will do anything for them (Hughes & Badley, 2022). Once I became a parent myself, I felt my professional perspective shift; I began to listen with increased attention when a parent became upset or frustrated with the school, with me, or even with their own child. I soon realized that when I offered empathy as a parent to a parent, the exchanges felt smoother and our teacher to parent connection was strengthened. I do recognize that whether a teacher is a parent or not, all teachers can learn to listen and shift our perspectives in new ways when we partner with parents and address their concerns.

It is critical to acknowledge that there are a multitude of challenges that can prevent parents from diving into their child's school community. Work schedules, language challenges, transportation issues, childcare needs, or simply not knowing how to gain access to a school can function as barriers. Regular communications and consistent invitations for involvement are recommended to strengthen parent, guardian, and teacher collaboration (Luckner & Rudolph, 2009). Making consistent efforts to connect with parents to solve problems, whether the problems involve their child or a school issue, can lead to potential solutions. In an ideal partnership, teachers view parents as fellow collaborators, rather than as a threat or annoyance. And as I've experienced firsthand, when parents are invited into schools as members of the team, as partners and collaborators, they often show up as superstar fundraisers and classroom volunteers. Parent involvement varies from district to district and school to school, however, integrating parents and guardians into a school community and tapping into their skillsets affirms parental assets not only for their child's education but for the greater purpose of K-12 schools.

Collaboration as Strength

Educator Carol Ann Tomlinson frames teaching as "the rare profession that allows its practitioners to model a world that dignifies—lifts up—all its members" (2015, p. 74). Tomlinson advocates for classrooms where teachers and students learn together to be completely human as the best versions of themselves. For collaborative success, it is essential to honor the individual as well as the team; learning and collaborating alongside others can be a professional asset. By nature, teachers are giving and selfless, so much so that we can be hyper-focused on students, resulting in having little time to think about ourselves. Thus, providing space for teachers to articulate their knowledge, experiences, and beliefs as collaborative partners becomes essential for productive collegial exchanges and school decision-making. As our world continues to evolve, it feels increasingly important to equip teachers with skills for collaboration. Basketball coach John Wooden once said, "The best players don't always make the best team ... a gifted player, or players who are not team players will ultimately hurt the team" (Wooden & Jamison, 1997, p. 74). I suggest we take the necessary steps to develop our collaborative skills for the good of our students and our educational teams.

Pause and Reflect

1. Name a time you have successfully collaborated with colleagues? How did you feel after the experience?
2. Recall a time that you made efforts to collaborate with colleagues and encountered challenges? How did you feel and respond? What did you learn about collaboration?
3. Does collaboration intimidate you? If so, consider why.
4. Take the time to set two to three manageable goals that demonstrate a commitment to developing active listening skills.
5. What collaborative activities can you implement in your classroom to foster increased student connections and nurture students' collaborative skills?

References

Aguilar, E. (2018). *Onward: Cultivating emotional resilience in educators.* Jossey-Bass.

Agvanyim, J. I. (2015). *The five principles of collaboration: Applying trust, respect, willingness, empowerment, and effective communication to human relationships.* iUniverse.

Aruda, W. (2023). How to show you are a leader at work. *Forbes.* https://www.forbes.com/sites/williamarruda/2023/10/10/how-to-show-you-are-a-leader-at-work/?sh=3fe7b7b9161f

Association for Middle Level Education (2023). Soft skills: Preparing kids for life after school. https://www.amle.org/soft-skills-preparing-kids-for-life-after-school/

Brooks, D. (2023). The essential skills for being human. *The New York Times.* https://www.nytimes.com/2023/10/19/opinion/social-skills-connection.html?searchResultPosition=1

Cheatham, J. P., Lim, E., & Williams, C. (2023). I teach educators how to change their minds. Here's how. *Education Week.* https://www.edweek.org/leadership/opinion-i-teach-educators-how-to-change-their-minds-hereshow/2023/09?utm_source=nl&utm_medium=eml&utm_campaign=eu&M=7827259&UUID=ed1e922 5cf4ea4152b58183549c88248&T=10408136

Feiman-Nemser, S., & Schussler, D. L. (2010). Defining, developing, and assessing dispositions: A cross-case analysis. In P. C. Murrell, M. E. Diez, S. Feiman-Nemser, & D. L. Schussler (Eds.), *Teaching as moral practice: Defining, developing, and assessing professional dispositions in teacher education* (pp. 177–201). Harvard Education Press.

Fleming, P., & Foster, E. (2022). A higher standard for professional learning. *Principal, 102*(2), 20–23. https://www.naesp.org/resource/a-higher-standard-for-professional-learning/

Gordon, G. (2020). *The joyful teacher.* Heinemann.

Hughes, M. C., & Badley, K. (2022). *Joyful resilience as educational practice: Transforming challenges into opportunities.* Taylor & Francis. https://doi.org/10.4324/9781003124429

Hurt, K. J. (2021). We need servant leaders now more than ever. *Servant Leadership: Theory & Practice, 8*(1), 1.

Johnston, D. K., Duvernoy, R., McGill, P., & Will, J. F. (2009). Educating teachers together: Teachers as learners, talkers, and collaborators. *Theory into Practice, 35*(3), 173–178.

Jones, L. (2021). The power of teacher collaboration. *Teaching Channel.* https://www.teachingchannel.com/k12-hub/blog/teacher-collaboration/

Knight, J. (2021). Hey instructional coach, what do you do? *Educational Leadership, 79*(1), 80–81. https://www.ascd.org/el/articles/the-learning-zone-hey-instructional-coach-what-do-you-do

Leana, C. R. (2011). The missing link in school reform, *Stanford Social Innovation Review, Fall,* 30–35. https://ssir.org/articles/entry/the_missing_link_in_school_reform

Levin, B. B., & Schrum, L. (2017). *Every teacher a leader. Developing the needed dispositions, knowledge, and skills for teacher leadership.* Corwin.

Little, G. F. (2022). Communities of practice encourage collective learning. *Principal, 102*(2), 16–19. https://www.naesp.org/resource/communities-of-practice-encourage-collective-learning/

Luckner, J., & Rudolph, S. (2009). *Teach well, live well.* Corwin.

Mathisen, J. (2022). The power of gifts from supervisors who share. In M. C. Hughes, & K. Badley (Eds.), *Joyful resilience as educational practice: Transforming teaching challenges into opportunities* (pp. 80–89). Taylor & Francis.

McCormick, M. D. (2022). Leverage your personality type. *Principal, 102*(2). https://www.naesp.org/resource/leverage-your-personality-type/

Murphy, I. P. (2022). Nurture relationship to deal with "difficult" personalities. *Principal, 102*(2), 40–42. https://www.naesp.org/resource/nurture-relationships-to-deal-with-difficult-personalities/

Northouse, P. G. (2021). *Leadership: Theory and practice* (9th ed.). Sage.

Tomlinson, C. A. (2015). Being human in the classroom. *Educational Leadership, 72*(2), 74–77. https://www.ascd.org/el/articles/being-human-in-the-classroom

Wenzel, A., & Roberts, J. (2014). Coaching teacher dispositions. *Association for Middle Level Education Magazine.* https://www.amle.org/coaching-teacher-dispositions/

Wooden, J., & Jamison, S. (1997). *Wooden: A lifetime of observations and reflections on and off the court.* Contemporary Books.

11

Courage

Courage Explained

Soon after new teachers experience the first days in their first teaching positions, they discover that courage must be added to their professional repertoire. Previous chapters in this book have highlighted the significance of dispositions or, as I like to call them, a teacher's greatest strength. In addition, earlier chapters underscored the multitude of professional responsibilities and heavy burdens that teachers carry. Much of the time, teachers bear professional obligations quietly and, as a result, teachers must develop and possess courage to persevere, withstand adversity, and navigate challenges. Courage requires moving from self-awareness to action with intentional effort. When teachers choose to nurture the disposition of courage and when they choose to act with courage, they may share a story, decision, or moment of courage; as a result, they also strengthen their aptitude for courage. Doing so can cultivate routines and habits of courage *and* when this occurs, teachers feel empowered and may pass the feeling on to our students.

Courage encompasses "mental and moral strength to persevere and withstand danger, fear, or difficulty" (Merriam-Webster, 2023). There are often dangerous situations on school campuses such as school shootings, physical fights, or targeted threats toward students or teachers. Thankfully, in most schools, there isn't extreme daily danger; however, an increasing need

DOI: 10.4324/9781003379539-11

persists for educators to muster up mental and moral strength to withstand professional challenges. In many countries around the world, when parents send their kids off on the bus or drop them off at elementary, junior high, or high school, the school and teachers assume the parental or guardian role; Latin for "in place of the parent," *in loco parentis*, refers to taking on parental responsibilities and allowing schools to act in the best interests of its students. This translates to courageous care. Teachers need a measure of courage, of guts, resolve, and strength of character to embrace the daily work that teaching requires. I personally recall days and weeks in my career when I had to summon a dose (sometimes a cup or gallon) of courage to respond to a disgruntled colleague, search trash cans after an anonymous campus bomb threat, or comfort a grieving student after a family member had passed away. While synonyms for courage include bravery and valor, it is worth noting that the Latin origin of the word courage comes from *cor* which means heart. As we explore the disposition of courage, we are also striving to strengthen our professional skills and hearts.

Teacher Bruises

As noted in earlier chapters, dispositions fuel us, are life-giving, and they shine a light on the intellectual work and heart work teaching necessitates. Although there are wonderful occasions for joy in our classrooms (see Chapter 13 on celebration and joy), anyone who has spent time in schools knows that K-12 classrooms are all-consuming and teachers sometimes feel a bit bruised and buried by their workloads. As I pondered potential links between the disposition of courage and this type of bruising, I was surprised to find synonyms for bruising that include burdensome, stressful, and exhausting. Do you ever feel this type of bruising as a teacher? I know I have from time to time.

One of my first professional bruises occurred in 1995. In April of that year, two individuals, Timothy McVeigh and Terry Nichols, bombed the Alfred P. Murrah Federal Building in Oklahoma City. Over 150 people were killed and almost

700 people were injured. A few days after this traumatic event, I hosted seventh-grade parents in my junior high classroom for an annual open house. As parents wandered in and out of my classroom looking at student work on display, one parent introduced herself as Frank's mom (a pseudonym). Frank's mom politely, yet passionately, shared that she was incredibly disappointed that I hadn't addressed or discussed the Oklahoma City Bombing with her child's English class. I was humbled and also deeply embarrassed by the encounter—I felt the impact to my core. To this day, I still feel a pit in my stomach when I think about that conversation with Frank's mom. The bruising I felt made a long-lasting imprint on my heart and mind; subsequently, I garnered self-awareness from the encounter and became increasingly willing to create space for students (whether they were in junior high, high school, or college) to dialogue about difficult topics and current events. Although, I was deeply affected by the conversation with Frank's mom, I was also energized to take more risks to address difficult topics in my classroom in subsequent years. This professional memory serves as a stand-out moment for me, a significant professional experience that prompted me to adopt a posture of courage to continue growing and learning professionally.

Throughout my career, like many of you, I recall the shock and grief associated with other monumental local, national, and global events: the terror attacks of 9/11, school shootings such as Columbine, and even California's Proposition 227. Proposition 227 stands out as a significant teachable moment in my professional journey. In 1998, this proposition became a state ballot initiative in favor of English only K-12 instruction that significantly changed how Limited English Proficient or second language learners were taught. The proposition passed, essentially eliminated bilingual instruction, and marginalized the Latinx population. I was a high school administrator at the time and I distinctly remember angry students walking out of classes in response to the election results. Deciding to honor students and their voices when they decided to protest in the neighborhood adjacent to our school, my administrative team chose to march alongside students as they took action.

Historical events like these prompt educators to tap into courage and respond to our students with care. More recently, educators were faced with student concerns and questions related to the attacks on the United States' Capitol on January 6, 2021. When I heard the news, I quickly responded by texting my elementary and secondary student teachers to check in on them, express support, and send a few teacher resources to help them think through how they could initiate and frame discussions with their own students in the subsequent days. Events such as this compel educators to find an extra measure of courage and even some humility as they respond. With today's complex political and social landscapes, teachers must be willing to address their own biases and privilege. As a result, I have purposely sought out professional resources and readings to help me engage in uncomfortable conversations that will help me interact with my students; my colleagues and I have also made increased efforts to lean in to listen and to understand. I confess that I am certainly not an expert for how to initiate classroom conversations like these, but thanks to some inner courage, I am not afraid to try. In addition, I have learned to recognize and name when I don't know something or don't understand a student's story, or a colleague's story, or their experiences. In these instances, I find that I must recognize my own privilege, acknowledge that I am a work in progress, and remain open to learning and growing which, in full transparency, isn't easy and requires courage.

Commit to Courage

I humbly confess that elementary and secondary student teachers, and pre-service professors like me, are often nervous, ill-equipped, and unsure of how to respond or even process real-time events such as those on January 6; nevertheless, teachers have a responsibility to do so. To add additional context, I'll remind us once again of twentieth-century philosopher John Dewey's vision of viewing education for the common good. Dewey advocated for public schools as venues to develop moral, democratic citizens.

He argued that teachers must cultivate dispositions and attitudes necessary for individual and societal growth (Dewey, 2005; Meadows, 2006). Teaching, much like nursing and other service fields, is traditionally considered a profession that works for the higher good. Teachers and nurses alike commit to serving and learning a unique set of skills, as well as honoring a professional code of ethics and core values (Ryan et al., 2016). It is important to recognize that even with shared values and a shared commitment, there is no guarantee that there won't be conflict in the workplace. Teachers know from experience that they will face struggles; when core values conflict with each other, teachers can get caught in the middle of a frustrated parent, a new policy about homework, or a curricular decision. These conflicts test teachers and require a measure of inner courage.

In the United States today, as the public is inundated with and exposed to exhaustive political rhetoric and a "facts vs. fake news" climate, teachers need to create classroom opportunities for students to engage in active reflection and inquiry. Offering a constructivist approach for meaning-making (Ryan et al., 2016), my faculty colleagues and I prioritize modeling and making room for education students to engage in dialogue related to difficult topics. We encourage student teachers to use visual images and concrete objects as springboard for dialogue. We also encourage them, often imperfectly, to recognize their biases and privilege, engage in anti-racist practices, and frame questions where their own students can think for themselves, weigh arguments, and sift through complex circumstances. We want our future teachers to find their inner voices, take risks, and respond in love to challenging and often traumatic life events. In order to do so, new and veteran teachers must remain open to being problem solvers who are willing to seek out help and resources from colleagues, counselors, parents, and administration. When teachers choose to teach in K-12 schools, we sign up with our core values and our moral compasses that include thinking through the dispositions and postures that we model and display to our students: empathy, resilience, gratitude to name a few are postures and behaviors that inform our classroom practice. Moreover, teachers have or *get to have* the unique honor to create brave and neutral spaces for dialogue, hard questions, and student engagement. The key word here is *get*—teachers *get* to experience, *get* to dive into, and *get* to foster opportunities where students can ask questions, wrestle with big ideas, and rethink their own moral compasses.

In 2017, the chief program academic officer of Expeditionary Learning School in Massachusetts framed courage as "differentiated courage" proposing that there are different kinds of courage. He suggested that individuals have more courage in certain areas and less in others (Berger, pp. 15). For instance, a student may display courage when they recite a poem in front of the class from memory, while another student may convey courage when they raise their hand to ask a question, or yet another student may disagree with another student during a group discussion. Recognizing that courage manifests itself in students in different ways illuminates the responsibility teachers have to empower students (and ourselves) with the disposition of courage.

The disposition of courage can be misunderstood because it is often associated with dramatic moments or grandiose experiences. Teachers activate inner courage in both simple and complex ways when they show up for students every day: to teach creatively, to meet with frustrated parents, to defend a curricular decision, or troubleshoot ways to help a struggling student. Author MaryAnn Radmacher suggests offering encouragement and inspiration to reshape the idea of courage with a focus on the ordinary. From speaking up to listening more in order to embrace change, Radmacher insists that courage can appear in subtle and unconventional ways (2022). Everyday courage, coined by educational consultant Cathy Lassiter, is required to face daily educational challenges; when schools need to raise test courses, address issues of equity, or challenge the status quo, courage is required. This type of courage includes the moral courage, intellectual courage, disciplined courage, and empathetic courage that teaching necessitates (2017). Everyday courage is a vital professional pre-requisite that intentionally leverages teacher bravery and links both the intellect and the heart.

Courage in Action

Practicing courage is necessary for educators to make decisions, face challenges, and persist in the profession (Palmer, 2000). Returning to the events of January 6, I recall a student teacher named Julie (a pseudonym), divulging to me that her students were quite upset when they learned about January 6. Julie's students were eager to make sense of the events on January 6 through discussion, writing, and critical thinking activities. Julie wanted to be honest with students about her own thoughts and reactions so she could cultivate students' trust. When she acknowledged that she didn't have all the answers, her high school students gained a sense of confidence as they wrestled with a pivotal moment in history. Additionally, presenting unbiased facts and posing open-ended questions helped Julie's students unpack their feelings in a non-threatening, non-confrontational manner. Julie boldly and masterfully modeled courage and risk-taking, both implicitly and explicitly, early in her teaching career and during a significant time in US history.

When those around us display courage, like Julie did, it becomes easier for others to be courageous (Wormeli, 2015). Whether we ask for help from colleagues, advocate for a new school program, or create a challenging and relevant unit plan, we demonstrate courage. Similar to so many other dispositions, displaying courage becomes contagious encouraging others to be brave. Growing and evolving professionally, with courage, can actually strengthen our professional outlook and our school communities (Tomlin, 2021). It takes courage to face the daily challenges, as well as the additional heavy lifting when change is required in schools. Whether teachers are discussing a new bell schedule, supporting struggling students, taking a stand at a school board meeting, or learning to teach remotely during a pandemic, they tap into their inner wells of courage.

Educators recognize that the pandemic highlighted disparities, learning gaps, and issues of inequity and access that necessitated a daily dose of courage to keep pushing through; yet, through the pandemic, teachers persisted, discovered, and demonstrated courage just by showing up. Reflecting back to the start of the pandemic, expectations of and for teachers will never be the same. The pandemic uncovered new stressors that required more than the "pick yourself up by the bootstraps" kind of courage. Acknowledging that teachers stay in the profession because they have a deep love for students and teaching, it is critical to also recognize that teachers typically choose to leave the profession because of its stressors (Loewus, 2021). Once again, it is a worthy and courageous goal to prompt schools to address how to best support a teacher's well-being. The way teachers feel about their work at the end of the day truly matters for both student and teacher success (Stark et al., 2022).

K-12 teachers and college faculty don't have all the answers for our students, for the educational system, or for our profession, nor should we be expected to provide them. As presented in Chapter 9, cultivating and creating safe, inclusive spaces for dialogue, inquiry, and meaning-making in the classroom develops students as critical thinkers and strong moral citizens. This has a ripple effect, impacts us all, and requires courage; most of the time it requires heaps of courage! Let me repeat this for emphasis: *teaching requires courage*! It takes courage to get up each morning, to show up for students, and to teach day in and day out. Of particular significance, dispositions like courage, inform our actions. When intentionally practiced, dispositions inspire additional practice opportunities that can result in habitual change (Hughes, 2018). When teachers choose to hone in and harness a disposition like courage, the intentional choice leads to action and increased inner courage. I credit Frank's mom many years ago for demonstrating courage when she approached me about the Oklahoma City Bombing. The experience was humbling and gave me a nudge or a swift kick, depending on how you look at it, to move forward and capitalize on the experience in my own practice. When teachers make the most of teachable moments like these, we foster confidence in ourselves and demonstrate courage to our colleagues and students. Likewise, on a recent podcast, Brene´ Brown thoughtfully discussed building brave spaces (2022); she also promoted tapping into deep listening skills, curiosity, and empathy to make room for courageous conversations which is what teachers do each and every day.

Courage to Inspire

The classroom is a place where teachers pour into students; teachers share, model, and shape. I recall a dear colleague once sharing with me that if schools everywhere are going to claim to be safe and inclusive then teachers need to be creative and courageous. I believe my colleague is correct. We are called to invite courage into the classroom for learning, as well as for facing life's challenges. I appreciate Kobi Yamada's children's book, *What Do You Do with a Problem?* (2016); Yamada's book thoughtfully addresses problems as unexpected nuisances, worries, and scary things. The main character, a boy, sees a problem in front of him and gears up to tackle the problem with courage. Discovering that the problem provides an opportunity to grow and demonstrate courage, the boy realizes he shouldn't be afraid of problems but instead should embrace them as opportunities for good. Another thoughtful but very different book, *Being Mortal*, written by physician Atul Gawande, addresses the strengths and flaws found in death, aging, and medicine. He frames courage as, "strength in the face of knowledge of what is to be feared or hoped" identifying two kinds of courage when facing aging and sickness (2017, p. 232). The first type of courage calls for facing mortality and truth; the second summons courage to act on the truth. Although classroom courage feels less extreme than a physician's courage needed for life and death decision-making, there is a distinct connection between the inner courage that both professionals need; teachers and physicians routinely confront a plethora of joys and challenging realities in the workplace and according to Gawande, courage gives us the strength we need to continue to persevere (Gawande, 2017).

Educators can seek to amplify the disposition of courage: we can share literature, personal stories, anecdotes, new curriculum, and strategies to inspire courage. We can summon courage as we make committee decisions, interact with students and colleagues, and address school-wide concerns. My colleague, Jenna (a pseudonym), once shared with me that when she taps into her own well of inner courage, she discovers great strength that produces glimmers of light and hope. Whether this type of light is from a sunrise or a sunset, or is seen through a window or a cracked door, the image offers those who see it hope and possibility. As we make daily professional decisions that require different degrees of courage, I invite you to reflect on the disposition of courage and intentionally share examples of courage with your students. Let's courageously shine our light to invigorate our practice and inspire our students. Subsequently, courage leads us to the disposition of hope in the next chapter (thanks Jenna).

Pause and Reflect

1. Do you view teaching as courageous work? Why or why not?
2. When have you demonstrated professional courage as a teacher and decision-maker?
3. Recall a personal story that personifies when you have demonstrated courage. Challenge yourself to share this story with your students and pay close attention to their responses.
4. Reflect on the ways that you were able to develop and exhibit courage during the pandemic.
5. How does the disposition of courage stimulate your interest in the other dispositions explored in *Dispositions Are a Teacher's Greatest Strength*?

References

Berger, R. (2017). The importance of academic courage. Edutopia. https://www.edutopia.org/article/importance-academic-courage

Brown, B.. (2022). Brene´ & Barrett on building brave spaces [Audio podcast episode]. https://brenebrown.com/podcast/building-brave-spaces/

Dewey, J. (2005). *Democracy and education*. Barnes and Noble Inc.

Gawande, A. (2017). *Being mortal*. Metropolitan Publishers.

Hughes, M. C. (2018). Dispositions: Real time active practice. *International Christian Teacher Education Journal, 13*(2). https://digitalcommons. georgefox.edu/icctej/vol13/iss2/7/

Lassiter, C. J. (2017). The courage to lead: Activating four types of courage for success. *Instructional Leader 30 (3)*. https://www.tepsa.org/ resource/the-courage-to-lead-activating-four-types-of-courage-for-success/

Loewus, L. (2021). Why teachers leave–or don't: A look at the numbers. https://www.pacesconnection.com/g/aces-in-education/blog/ why-teachers-leave-or-don-t-a-look-at-the-numbers-edweek-org

Meadows, E. (2006). Preparing teachers to be curious, open minded and actively reflective: Dewey's ideas reconsidered. *Action in Teacher Education, 28*(2), 4–14.

Merriam-Webster (2023). Courage. *In Merriam-Webster.com Dictionary*. https://www.merriam-webster.com/dictionary/courage?src= search-dict-box

Palmer, P. (2000). *The courage to teach*. Jossey-Bass.

Radmacher, A. (2022). *Courage doesn't always roar and sometimes is does: Re-defining courage with daily inspirations*. Conari Press.

Ryan, K., Cooper, J. M., & Mason-Bolick, C. (2016). *Those who can, teach*. Cengage Learning.

Stark, K., Daulat, N., & King, S. (2022). A vision for teachers' emotional well-being. *Phi Delta Kappan, 103*(5), 24–30. https://doi. org/10.1177/00317217221079975

Tomlin, D. (2021). Courageous construction in the middle grades. *Association for Middle Level Education*. https://www.amle.org/ courageous-construction-in-the-middle-grades/

Wormeli, R. (2015). The courage it takes. *Association for Middle Level Educators, 4*(2). https://www.amle.org/the-courage-it-takes/

Yamada, K. (2016). *What do you do with a problem?* Compendium.

12

Hope

Why Hope?

When I initially dove into reading and learning about the disposition of hope, I wondered how I could hold onto hope and share hope with my community: my students, my family, my neighbors, and my friends. After experiencing multiple natural disasters in my community (see Chapter 6 on resilience), examining hope—often framed as a wish or desire for things to change for the better—felt timely. I was motivated to consider where and when teachers find hope in their classrooms amidst lockdown drills, students' mental health challenges, and even after natural disasters. Because teachers serve on the frontlines as first responders that care, troubleshoot, and help students every day, I wondered how teachers confront difficult and unexpected circumstances with hope. Could teachers even find the time and space to recognize hope in the middle of the day-to-day busyness and stress? Additionally, I questioned how new and veteran teachers discover hope in their teaching, in classrooms, with colleagues, and in the faces of their students.

Ironically, I started writing and thinking about hope when the pandemic arrived. Much like most of the world, the outbreak jolted my family, local community, and country. Quite honestly, the pandemic challenged my personal beliefs about hope. Hope in a traditional sense, provides inspiration and belief that you and I will make it through. Unfortunately, there was no ending point

DOI: 10.4324/9781003379539-12

or roadmap at the onset of the pandemic and as a result many educators felt constant confusion and even despair. Personally, in the middle of the pandemic's unusual circumstances, I genuinely wondered if hope could be found. In hindsight, I now know that the pandemic provided a unique opportunity for renewed perspective, professional development, and personal growth. I *hope* you will find *hope* as you read this chapter.

The disposition of hope indicates optimism, confidence, courage, promise, or potential. The disposition of hope can be studied as a noun, yet, it cannot be overlooked as a verb. Hope as a verb expects, anticipates, wishes, yearns, or longs for something. Hope urges people, like you and me, to trust. Hope and the act of waiting is often a decision; we are obligated to pause, be patient, anticipate, and discover hope as we wait or yearn to move forward.

Historically, Christian faith has recognized hope in Jesus Christ, as seen most prominently on Easter weekend, when Christians go from despair on Good Friday to waiting for Christ's return and triumphant rise from death on Sunday (Keller, 2021). Most religious or spiritual practices, like Christianity, point to a form of hope whether it is found in relationships, community, moral codes, or rituals. Hope frequently appears as a positive outcome from adversity or challenging circumstances; "It takes courage and trust in the unseen to press on during a life-threatening storm" (Miller, 2020, p. 219).

Increasing responsibilities for teachers in schools, safety concerns, and political distractions have exposed the increased need for educators to find hope in times of angst as well as in the waiting. Author and educator Erin Gruwell addresses the need for hope in her book, *Teaching Hope*. Gruwell's collection of realistic teacher stories acknowledge the unique challenges found in the ebb and flow of the school year: from the anticipation on the first day of the school year to the disenchantment teachers can feel mid-year, to the elation and accomplishment teachers experience at the end of the school year, teachers need to find and feel hope as professionals (2009). Educators need to seek hope and fight for hope more than ever before as they grapple with challenging circumstances in schools. Choosing hope can affirm a teacher's work in the classroom as well as their professional calling.

Seek Hope

When I picture hope, I often see hope in a variety of contexts. I picture landscapes and nature found in the mountains or sunset scenes. These settings allow me to take a deep breath to observe nature's awe and beauty. I also find hope when I experience a friend's smile or hear laughter. A smile and laughter can lighten a mood, lift spirits, and provide perspective. Similarly hope can also be found in the classroom. This type of hope occurs when a student teacher experiences an "ah-ha" or "lightbulb moment," or when the learning clicks and a young student discovers something new. In addition, I find that when I am able to mentor or guide a colleague through a professional decision, I feel hope-filled. I see and experience additional glimpses of hope when my colleagues and I face problems together and search for solutions. Hope shines in and through these distinct contexts and circumstances.

I also see hope in a child's naivety and optimism. I distinctly remember when I was young, when I felt invincible and thought I could tackle any challenge placed before me. This type of hope felt full of infectious joy. When life feels heavy and uncertain, I try to remember and revisit this innocent optimism and childlike perspective. Similarly, Bryan Goodwin, an educational writer and researcher, recognizes that a romantic view of teaching changes lives and is often overshadowed with the discovery of how stressful and difficult teaching can be. He claims that new teachers are works in progress, still developing, and that the hope found in a student teacher's rose-colored glasses is needed for the profession (2019). Grounded in romanticism, this perspective focuses on the needs of individual students and also highlights student curiosity as a means to encourage development (Ryan et al., 2016). In pre-service programs, faculty endeavor to balance romantic idealism for the profession alongside the realities and tensions inherent in the profession.

A few years ago, I sat at a memorial service for a friend who passed away far too young. I listened to Jon, my friend's oldest son (a pseudonym), share about the pain of watching his mom die a cruel death from an unrelenting disease. Jon spoke of the tension he felt caring for his mom, his anger, his sadness and frustration, however, he also admitted that recognizing these tensions led him to hope. Upon reflection, he recognized that he needed to look in the rearview mirror at the past. Revisiting the hardships that he encountered through his mom's illness gave him glimmers of hope to go on, to look forward, and to move ahead. By looking in the rearview mirror, Jon was able to recognize the good, the joys, the laughter, and the sweet memories that he had enjoyed with his mom—even during her painstaking illness. Jon's authentic testimony affirmed the disposition of hope and the notion that hope flourishes even through difficult circumstances.

Hurdles and joys like Jon experienced can carry us through challenging moments and seasons. Author Tim Keller validates the notion that we can choose optimism and hope when we face difficulties. He notes that through arduous, and often dark times, even a global pandemic, hope reveals itself (2021). Similarly, author Annie Downs (2016) argues that there is a connection between beauty and perseverance that exposes hope and motivates a person to keep going. She points to the idea that beauty can move us forward, inspire us to persevere, push us to dig deep, and forge ahead. Educator Phyllis Fagell affirms this thinking, "We can't alter our current reality, but we can recognize that it's temporary and situational, and choose to preserve our optimism and relationships and emerge stronger together" (2020, p. 46). Although the pandemic brought teachers excess stress, we also witnessed beauty, perseverance, and optimism throughout the unexpected season. Teachers went the extra mile to drop off books at students' houses, they emailed and called parents, taught creatively, and even wore costumes to teach remotely. These gestures fueled teachers and at the same time gifted a glimmer of hope to students. There truly is no greater teacher reward than sharing a disposition like hope with students and then seeing the disposition flourish within the students and classroom.

Hopeful Strategies

I find that I feel hopeful when I choose to view hope as an oppor-tunity to learn and grow. For new teachers to become great teachers, they must be encouraged to take risks, make mistakes, and accept uncertainty (France, 2019). Individually and collectively, we can choose to set our sights on hope and transfer an attitude of hope to our students. When our classrooms feel filled with a lack of hope due to challenging circumstances, we can choose to embrace, seek, frame, and identify hope with students and colleagues. I recommend five hopeful and practical strategies for educators. First, I suggest that we first search for hope. As teachers, we can intentionally reflect and ask ourselves where we see, find, and discover hope in our teaching, at our schools, with our students and colleagues. We can seek to identify hope in remote learning settings. We can also intentionally search for hope-filled moments in our physical classrooms. Early on in the pandemic, I routinely observed student teachers teaching remotely. During each of the remote observations, I was struck by the level of patience I witnessed, the extensive use of wait time, and the level of com-passion and care heard in each student teacher's voice. Observing student teachers in such a challenging environment highlighted the unexpected skills and dispositions that they were developing despite their circumstances. These observations gave me hope, as well as underscored student teachers' responses to their circumstances as an explicit conduit toward hope. Ironically, the difficulties that all teachers experienced teaching remotely during the pandemic also produced a format for teachers from all over the world to connect and collaborate more easily with each other. Teaching during the pandemic was extremely overwhelming, yet so many educators chose to frame and reframe their challenges as opportunities for growth; as a result they were able to inspire hope in their students.

A second suggestion to foster hope involves using hope-filled language. The use of hopeful words can inspire hope (and even joy). Words link us, touch us and yes, they sometimes hurt us, but reframing our communications and conversations around hope can foster and even reset our classroom tone. Intentionally using vocabulary that displays hope as well as what we expect and hope for in others can nurture hope. Educational advocate Jimmy Casas recommends that teachers bring their best selves to school each day; he encourages living out enthusiastic excellence in our work (Casas, 2020). We can honor our professionalism and set examples of excellence for students when we explicitly identify hope. Choosing hopeful vocabulary can elevate our conversations and speech (Spencer, 2018); using hope-filled language can stimulate hope within us and within our students. For instance, I can choose to describe a student as lazy or disinterested *or* I can decide to reframe my description of the same student with hopeful language such as, "The student is not yet engaged." I might also say, "I am eager to do some detective work to uncover what motivates the student."

School communities and teachers can choose to offer hope and be conduits of hope for students (Casas, 2020). Intentionally, seeking to grow the disposition of hope in practice can help teachers build self-awareness around hope for themselves and their students. Researcher Angela Duckworth suggests putting forth efforts to cultivate a hopeful spirit (2016). Carol Ann Tomlinson affirms Duckworth's recommendation and suggests engaging in regular collegial conversations about teaching to nourish and fuel professional growth (2019). Admittedly, not all conversations about teaching are hope-filled; however, teachers can choose to use positive language and framing to focus on the positive. Teachers have the power to choose the place from where they teach as well as what they teach toward (Moreno, 2019; Palmer, 2007). Collectively and intentionally, we can steer our conversations and responses, as well as our tone away from criticism so we can instead look toward hope.

Community is another suggestion for discovering hope; hope unites and bonds us and a united community can shine a light on hope. Throughout his career, children's television host, Mr. Rogers, urged his daily audience to look for the helpers, especially in challenging times (Neville, 2018). Rogers wasn't necessarily pointing to present day natural disasters, school shootings, or even pandemics, but his suggestion to seek out the helpers touches our hearts and reminds us of our human connections in times of crisis. Throughout the pandemic, I purposefully made the decision to start each of my classes with a specific question to gauge how each student was doing and feeling. I often asked students to share how they displayed self-care and where they found gratitude. Through the intentional questioning, I was reminded that when we are responsive to students and when we interact regularly with them, we can reinforce Nel Noddings' ethic of care (2003). Moreover, when students perceive a teacher's care, their motivation, engagement in class, and student to teacher connections grow, and even flourish (Milner, 2019; Shotsberger & Freytag, 2020). Efforts like these can also be framed as instances of hospitality referenced earlier in Chapter 9. Hospitality can actually provide a crucial and authentic opportunity for student learning and success; thus, making room for connection and relationship invites optimism and hope into a classroom and school community (Hoerr, 2014). In addition, giving students opportunities to hope—to see the possibility in learning, growing, and succeeding further stimulates hope in learners (Jensen, 2008).

Recognizing unexpected opportunities for hope is an additional recommendation for fostering hope. Parker Palmer, through his writings, consistently encourages teachers to look within to know themselves because "teaching holds a mirror to the soul" (2007, p. 3). As educators, we know that meaningful learning for students and teachers requires vulnerability, mistake-making, risk-taking, and a growth mindset. Today's research affirms that investing in teachers' humanity and risk-taking encourages, empowers, and motivates student learning and cultivates greater human connection (France, 2019). In the same way, Palmer notes that life's paradoxes are full of joy and complexity (2007); ultimately, when we choose to foster and develop dispositions like hope, the effort can amplify hope as we address life's paradoxes.

It is essential to name that seeking hope and finding hope is not just about staying positive; putting on an insincere happy face devalues the important work that teachers do. Hope isn't enough unless a teacher's well-being and health are attended to, therefore, acknowledging the challenging work that teachers engage in affirms and validates a teacher's humanity and their professional self. Cultivating school communities that talk the talk and walk the walk that value teachers as humans who have emotional ups and downs, gives teachers hope. When a school organization enthusiastically supports a teachers' well-being and promotes a healthy school culture, teachers feel hope-filled.

Conclusion

When we reflect, look into the rearview mirror, and look into the future, we have a choice to intentionally capitalize on the challenging circumstances we encounter as teachers; we can choose to use the unexpected circumstances to cultivate human connection, build bridges, and problem solve—or not. Similar to the other dispositions in this book, we must consistently practice hope with intention so hope can develop in us, fuel us, and keep us going.

At the onset of the pandemic, I crafted an impromptu reflection about my work as a professor of pre-service teachers. The words I wrote captured my thoughts and emotions at the beginning of the pandemic. Revisiting this reflection, I am reminded of the hope that students unknowingly foster and inspire in me:

I am a teacher of teachers and a person who is high touch, highly interactive, and extroverted. With that said, the last few weeks [at the start of the pandemic] have brought a deep sense of loss. One of my pre-service program's strengths is that we are deeply relational. Our Education Program strives to model building relationships with students starting in the first class meeting each new semester. We greet at the door, high five our students, and invite them into learning. Our team, and those before us, have built strong school, district, and community partnerships. In every education course we teach, we make efforts to demonstrate strategies that cultivate classroom community, value human connection, and model knowing and seeing our students and their individual stories. Remote learning, Facetimes and phone calls are necessary tools that we need and use at this time, yet, during this unusual season, I feel like we are letting our students down. I know personally and professionally that we don't have control over the current circumstances. Teachers are all doing their best. We are humbly reminded of the need for human proximity, sharing and creating laughter, demonstrating passion for content, and engaging in dialogue together in the same room—these things are missing and it stings. As our team moves forward—we still feel hopeful—we recognize, value, and are thankful for human contact more than ever and we can't wait to be back in our classrooms with students.

After putting these thoughts down on paper, I wondered how I could do better and be better for those in my life: my students, my family, my neighbors, and my circle of friends. I actually felt a spark of hope and renewal in me. I recognized that, as educators, we have the opportunity to transform how we behave and respond—one student and one classroom at a time. We can choose to frame our work, its significance, and our professional practice through a hope-filled lens. I find that choosing to write about the disposition of hope, gives me increased hope; and although much of the complex aftermath from the pandemic remains, shifting my perspective to hope actually stimulates new hope in me.

When asked in an interview to share her views on hope, poet Amanda Gorman responded, "I always believe that hope isn't something you possess, it's something you practice. It has to be earned. It has to be fought for ..." (Gorman, A.S.C., 2023). I wholeheartedly agree! Teachers can make an uncompromising decision to search for hope and to model hope. We can align our actions and moral commitments with the disposition of hope. As we grapple with the future, whether we are teaching remotely, organizing a fieldtrip for students, or high-fiving students at a school assembly, I enthusiastically propose that we commit to seek hope in relationships, hope in our students, hope in our colleagues, and hope in our school communities. Developing hope can help us discover unexpected gifts in our work. Hope gives us fuel for the future (Taulbert, 2006). Hope, we invite you into our classrooms and our hearts.

Pause and Reflect

1. What hope-filled language and phrases do you use in your classroom? How do students respond when you use this language?
2. Describe a time that you discovered a glimmer of hope through challenging professional circumstances? Did hope change your perspective?
3. How do the other dispositions explored in *Dispositions Are a Teacher's Greatest Strength* lead you to the disposition of hope?
4. Consider and look for hope-filled qualities and postures in your colleagues. Might you honor your colleagues by telling them about the hope that you see in them?
5. How can the disposition of hope affirm and elevate your professional practice?

References

Casas, J. (2020). *Live your excellence: Bring your best self to school every day.* Dave Burgess Consulting.

Downs, A. (2016). *Looking for lovely.* B and H Books.

Duckworth, A. (2016). *Grit: The power of passion and perseverance.* Simon and Schuster.

Fagell, P. (2020). How to build a resilient school community. *Association for Middle Level Education Magazine, 8*(4), 44–46. https://www.amle. org/how-to-build-a-resilient-school-community/

France, P. E. (2019). The value of vulnerability. *Educational Leadership, 77*(1), 78–82. https://www.ascd.org/el/articles/the-value-of-vulnerability

Goodwin, B. (2019). Keep the romance alive: How can we help teachers maintain a long-term love of their jobs? *Educational Leadership, 77*(1), 84–85. https://www.ascd.org/el/articles/keep-the-romance-alive

Gorman, A. S. (2023). *I always believe that hope isn't something you possess.* [Instagram @amandascgorman]. https://www.instagram.com/ amandascgorman/

Gruwell, E. (2009). *Teaching hope: Stories from the freedom writer teachers and Erin Gruwell*. Broadway Books.

Hoerr, T. R. (2014). Principal connection: Service vs. hospitality. *Educational Leadership, 71*(6), 88–91. https://www.ascd.org/el/articles/service-vs.-hospitality

Jensen, E. (2008). *Brain-based learning: The new paradigm of teaching* (2nd ed.). Corwin Press.

Keller, T. (2021). *Hope in times of fear*. Viking.

Miller, S. (2020). *Searching for certainty: Finding God in the disruptions of life*. Bethany House.

Milner, H. R. (2019). Confronting inequity: Lessons from pre-Brown teachers of color. *Educational Leadership, 76*(7), 89–90. https://www.ascd.org/el/articles/lessons-from-pre-brown-teachers

Moreno, R. (2019). How can we use dialogue to empower our students? *Association for Middle Level Education Magazine, 7*(4), 5–7. https://www.amle.org/how-can-we-use-dialogue-to-empower-our-students/

Neville, M. (Director). (2018). *Won't you be my neighbor*. [Film]. Focus Features.

Noddings, N. (2003). *Caring: A feminine approach to ethics and moral education*. University of California Press.

Palmer, P. (2007). *The courage to teach: Exploring the inner landscape of a teacher's life*. Jossey-Bass.

Ryan, K., Cooper, J. M., & Mason Bolick, C. (2016). *Those who can teach, teach*. Cengage Learning.

Shotsberger, P., & Freytag, C. (Eds.). (2020). *How shall we then care? A Christian educator's guide to caring for self, learners, colleagues and community*. Wipf and Stock.

Spencer, G. (2018). *Reframing the soul: How words transform our faith*. Leafwood Publishers.

Taulbert, C. L. (2006). *Eight habits of the heart for educators: Building strong school communities through timeless values*. Corwin.

Tomlinson, C. A. (2019). One to grow on/collegial conversations can fuel teacher growth. *Educational Leadership, 77*(3), 92–93. https://www.ascd.org/el/articles/collegial-conversations-can-fuel-teacher-growth

13

Celebration and Joy

Teachers Crave Joy

In the field of education, it is common knowledge that a significant number of novice teachers leave their positions within the first five years of teaching. In a 2019 study, half of teacher participants in public schools pondered leaving the profession because they felt an overwhelming sense of burnout for a multitude of reasons; being asked to do too much without compensation or support topped the list of reasons that teachers leave (Santoro, 2019).

People in general, not just teachers, need to feel appreciated and recognized. President Barack Obama noted in his documentary series, *Working*, that dignity means finding purpose in our work (Suh, 2023). Teachers truly want to engage in purposeful and productive work that adds value to others, especially in relation to their students' achievement, building strong classrooms, and developing strong school communities. Unfortunately, teachers often feel demoralized and frustrated when they are unable to engage in productive ways. When a teacher's resources have been used up or when teachers don't see the value in their work, they may believe their contributions are not possible anymore. Working conditions and curricular changes are contributors to this type of teacher discontent; changes in school leadership and compliance efforts also impact teacher dissatisfaction (Santoro, 2019). Making

DOI: 10.4324/9781003379539-13

efforts to understand why teachers choose to leave the profession inform how schools and districts can get teachers to stay (Santoro, 2019). Furthermore, examining the reasons for teacher dissatisfaction underscores learning how teachers can find increased joy in their work. Several decades ago, teacher dissatisfaction and retention issues inspired states and school districts in the United States to create mandatory mentoring programs to support new teachers through their first few years on the job. Such programs continue to offer peer mentoring with thoughtfully designed growth plans and goal-setting, as well as non-evaluative opportunities to strengthen teacher practice. Research shows that these efforts decreased teacher isolation and led to greater job satisfaction (Heider, 2005). I have witnessed firsthand how structured mentoring programs offer extensive support to new teachers in their first years of teaching; building new teacher confidence with a trusted mentor can empower and sustain teachers.

Creating Space and Contexts for Celebration and Joy

Recently, I picked up *Developing Assessment Capable Visible Learners Grades K-12: Maximizing Skill, Will and Thrill*, a book focused on developing learners for the sake of learning (Frey et al., 2018). The book's title caught my attention because of the word *thrill*, which, for me, implies that developing learners for the sake of learning is important. This book and its title inspired me to consider how we can frame (or reframe) our thinking to help students find and feel the thrill, the joy, and the celebration in learning as an engaging question and worthy goal for educators to pursue.

As I reflect on celebration and joy, I am reminded about my days as a student. In my early years as a student in elementary school, I found joy in completing tasks, taking and passing spelling tests, and connecting with friends at recess. I fondly remember days when I finished a book, passed an exam, performed in a play, or assisted a teacher after school. Each of these instances felt like a genuine accomplishment and produced inner joy. Additionally, I recall the times I earned an award on my high school tennis team or when I graduated from high school. These experiences prompted celebrations that sparked joy. Earning a bachelor's degree and teaching credential as well as attending graduate school were additional milestones that generated celebration and joy in me as a student and career professional. In full transparency, I was a good student, liked school, was a rule follower, and still am. It's in my DNA. At the same time, it isn't a surprise that a lot of students feel differently about school. Some students genuinely struggle to embrace school or their circumstances prevent it, and consequently, their school experiences do not resemble mine. Accordingly, celebration and joy can mean different things to different people, especially our students; because of this, I suggest that as we consider when and how we differentiate vocabulary lessons or math assessments for students, that we also mull over when and how our students can find joy in the classroom. What floats a student's boat? What stimulates a student's curiosity and spirit of inquiry? What makes a student want to learn more?

Curiously, even as I write this chapter, I see additional connections between the dispositions explored in *Dispositions Are a Teacher's Greatest Strength* and intrinsic and extrinsic motivation. Discovering what motivates students to ask questions, search for new information, or work to impress a teacher informs a teacher's methods and responses. I vividly remember my own children coming home from elementary school squealing and waving a ticket they were given at recess because they were caught doing something good on the playground. Every time this happened, their name was put in a jar for prizes from the principal. This small extrinsic reward made an impact on my own children; they were acknowledged for a positive behavior and the recognition improved their attitude and confidence. Even though my children were instantly happy and the recess tickets instances were heartwarming, I wonder how teachers can use motivation as a positive tool for celebration and joy. Every teacher has their own philosophy and toolbox to motivate students; however, intrinsic motivation is the more favorable outcome endorsed by educators. Despite this, it is important to acknowledge that extrinsic motivation plays a role in classrooms and impacts students in distinct ways (Durwin & Reese-Weber, 2017). Whether teachers advocate for intrinsic or extrinsic motivation in their classrooms, I imagine educators can agree that identifying what motivates individual students or a class of students can be great cause for celebration. According to Eric Jensen, when teachers nurture student confidence in learners through celebration, recognition, class parties, pep rallies, or performances, they empower students and actually feed the brain. Because emotions drive what people do and trigger chemical changes in our behaviors and moods, celebrations foster students' confidence and intrinsic motivation (2008). The feel-good chemicals that are produced in our bodies energize and empower learners. Notably, "learners in positive, joyful environments are likely to experience enhanced learning, memory, and self-esteem" which is an additional victory for students *and* teachers (Jensen, 2008, p. 99).

Teachers love to calendar upcoming events and celebrations, and they enjoy looking for opportunities to engage in classroom celebrations that produce joy. Whether it's in the form of a field trip, an award ceremony, or an "ah-ha" moment, teachers are their students' greatest champions; what's more, every student needs a champion who will recognize and celebrate student progress and milestones (TED, 2013). Often defined as "marking an anniversary, occasion or festivity" (Merriam-Webster, 2023), celebration denotes cheering for and recognizing students and classroom successes. The classroom is an obvious place to celebrate learning that sets the stage and precedent for joy! From small moments to big accomplishments, celebration produces smiles, and joy-filled moments. Inviting celebration into the classroom, building on student-teacher relationships, and sharing joy with intention generates additional capacity for celebration and joy. Intentional fun that is connected to learning outcomes can lead to joy and satisfaction for students and teachers. Prioritizing fun activities in lessons using unique teaching approaches elicits quality learning experiences and boosts student engagement (Thornhill & Badley, 2020, p. 140).

Joy produces "the emotion evoked by well-being, success or good fortune"; joy is "a source of or cause of delight" (Merriam-Webster, 2023). Finding opportunities for celebration fosters joy and elevates a classroom's ethos and culture. Additionally, in the last decade, research reveals that the brain is more receptive to learning when learning is joyful. Such findings increase a teacher's motivation to cultivate classroom joy (Costa & Kallick, 2014).

While exploring the disposition of celebration, I discovered that I kept returning to the disposition of joy; in response, I decided to focus on two dispositions: celebration *and* joy. From my perspective, it doesn't feel right to separate celebration and joy, because celebration and joy seem to find each other; they are intertwined like so many of the dispositions in this book. It feels challenging to examine celebration without joy or joy without celebration. Hence, I was inspired to consider how educators can capitalize on both celebration and joy in our classrooms. Curiously, New York School Superintendent Jennifer Gallagher promotes a similar mindset and notices links between courage, curiosity, and joy in secondary education (2023). Stating that joy is an underestimated educational resource, Gallagher advocates for increased joy for school change suggesting that teachers tap into courage in order to integrate joy and curiosity into learning. Revisit Chapters 2 and 11 to learn more about the dispositions of curiosity and courage.

Students are assigned to a clinical placement in a K-12 classroom in one of my undergraduate courses. The course functions as an ideal learning laboratory because students are reading and learning about elementary and secondary classrooms, professionalism, and the foundations of American education, while at the same time, that are interacting with students and a cooperating teacher. As students immerse themselves into K-12 classrooms, they begin to make connections to course readings and discussions. After a few weeks in their clinical placements, students are known to come to class exclaiming, "I have found my calling!" or "I love this! I love being with students!" These moments scream of celebration and joy when one of my students discovers their professional calling or links course readings, activities, and discussions to their clinical placement; they emanate pure joy *and* enthusiastic celebration ensues. In these instances, I also feel great inner joy and celebration. Observing and participating in these wonderful encounters that connect both the intellect and the heart are cause for celebration that further illuminates joy!

Teachers embrace classroom celebrations in a variety of ways: for perfect attendance, parent conferences, spring break, the seasons, birthdays, and the end of a semester. Teachers may celebrate strong collaboration among students in class, or they may plan culminating events, field trips, family nights, or recognition programs for students and their families. Whether celebrations are community celebrations or quiet individual celebrations, they make an impact.

Some of my fondest celebratory memories occur when I give out awards and honors to students. Whether I choose to recognize a top student in our education major or credit an undergraduate for their spirit of inquiry, students relish each celebration. What's more, celebration elevates both teachers' and students' moods. For instance, each semester in my introductory class, I publicly award certificates to students for a variety of reasons: for their thoughtful questions, teamwork, or can-do attitudes. As I enthusiastically (and sometimes dramatically) recognize each student, they typically blush a bit and smile. After all the awards are shared, I ask how the recognition made each student feel. In full transparency, a few students are embarrassed, but most students express surprise and gratitude for the personal recognition. Students are typically full of gratitude (refer to Chapter 7 for more on gratitude) because they were noticed and seen by me, their teacher. Once again, recognizing students boosts an individual's endorphins that stimulate learning (Jensen, 2008); there is physical payoff when students feel joy and success.

In the last few decades, when every child participant in a sport or theater production began receiving a trophy, society coined the term "trophy generation." Whether participants won or lost, awarding trophies to all participants can feel extreme; yet, praising students (and even colleagues) can be a powerful and productive tool for motivation, achievement, and confidence. Undoubtedly, research reveals that when people receive recognition, when they are celebrated, they increase productivity and engagement with others (Rath & Clifton, 2004). In contrast, insincere celebration can feel counterproductive or disingenuous.

Celebrate Humans

There are a multitude of classroom contexts for celebration that can lead to joy. More than ever, teachers, in their professional roles, are expected to recognize students as human beings and individuals. Most often, teachers celebrate student accomplishments as a natural part of the job; whether they pass a benchmark assessment or are caught doing something good. At the same time, it can be challenging to celebrate students who struggle or test a teacher's patience. Regardless, teachers can validate the stresses and struggles of students so they are seen as unique individuals who also see themselves (Egbert, 2020). Assessment opportunities can also help teachers build relationships with students that can also lead to celebrating students; and when teachers understand a student's areas of proficiency, areas for growth, and emotional needs, assessment can be viewed as an expression of love and care. "It [assessment] can also be a way to ensure we are giving students the tools and skills they need and perhaps even to look for gifts to bring to the table" (Torres, 2019, para 14). Author and educator Harro Van Brummelen affirms this thinking and promotes assessment that both supports and stimulates student learning as "assessment *for* learning and *as* learning" (2012, p. 89). He believes assessment "shapes students' dispositions, values, and attitudes" (Van Brummelen, 2012, p. 90). When teachers intentionally look to assess and celebrate the growth in students' behavior or students' academic progress, students glean the benefits. When students are seen as more than a test score or ranking, teachers are better able to support them, recognize their gifts, and celebrate them which further acknowledges the humanity of students as well as fosters their self-efficacy.

Teachers typically find joy in students' big accomplishments, but perhaps more importantly, they can choose to celebrate the small stuff or the smaller student victories. Possessing and sharing a joyful spirit can deepen when we choose to savor both the big and little moments of progress and growth in our classrooms. One of the larger celebratory events that my education department hosts annually is called the "Celebration of Teaching." This gathering includes our pre-service program's village of college faculty, staff, cooperating teachers, student teachers, principals, friends, and family members. At the event, student teachers share prepared speeches—or as I like to call them, "tales from the trenches"—from their student teaching experiences. They not only celebrate the significant accomplishment of completing their student teaching, but they also share the achievement with their support systems by recognizing their cooperating teachers, families, professors, and friends that helped them accomplish their goals. The "Celebration of Teaching" event joyfully brings our educational community together, celebrates all in attendance, and honors the gift of collective community; it truly takes a village to prepare a student teacher for their professional future. While this event is one example of an educational celebration, celebrating students can take many forms, big and small. I regularly remind my student teachers that celebration can come in the form of a parent phone call. In my experience, most teachers dread making parent phone calls. Nevertheless, I intentionally remind student teachers to call home as an act of celebration because phone calls are opportunities to share about student progress, learn about students, and create joy (yes, *create joy*). Parents may cringe, get angry at their child, or may be extremely disappointed in themselves when a teacher calls to report a student's missing assignment, poor student attitude, or misbehavior. Because of this, many of the teachers I know procrastinate calling home because they predict the dialogue might be uncomfortable; similarly, a parent's first thoughts when a teacher calls home may be, "Uh-oh, what did my child do?" because phone calls of celebration are typically rare. However, when a teacher calls home to say, "I love having X student in class" or "I noticed X student's writing and vocabulary use improved this week," a parent may

be pleasantly surprised. Years ago, I received a phone call of celebration for my junior high daughter. I not only appreciated that
the teacher made the effort to call, but I dropped everything to
celebrate and take my daughter out for ice-cream. I discovered
firsthand that when a teacher takes the time to call home for positive and productive reasons, their actions can result in a positive
interaction or small celebration at home. Educator Taylor Mali's
thinking aligns with my experience; he notes that calling parents
with praise for a child's classroom success results in the student
coming to class the next day with a bigger smile and a skip in their
step (2012, p. 35). Furthermore, "Recognition is most appreciated
and effective when it is individualized, specific, and deserved"
(Rath & Clifton, 2004, p. 62). A one-size-fits-all approach doesn't
work for all students, but specific, authentic, and meaningful recognition can make an impact and serve as a powerful motivator
for students (pp. 65–66).

Celebrate the Wins!

A colleague who teaches high school history once shared with
me that he felt discouraged after weeks of greeting lethargic,
uninterested students at his classroom door. After verbalizing his
frustration, one of his students told him that he [the teacher] was
the only teacher in the school that knew the student's name; the
student shared that he comes to school only for this particular
teacher; the interaction became a win, a teachable moment, and
a victory for both the student and the teacher. Educators can
look for and identify these types of wins with our students and
colleagues. One suggestion includes celebrating and acknowledging kindness, not in a patronizing way, but in an uplifting
way. Succinct and targeted statements such as, "your thoughtful-
ness inspires me" communicate kindness, uplift others, and may
lead to a little joy and perhaps celebration (Radmacher, 2022).
Simple efforts like these remind me that there are a number of
phrases I can use to instantly uplift a person's day. Language
such as, "I see your gifts" or "You are making a difference"
or "You inspire me" highlight a person's strengths, celebrate

progress, and even point to qualities of character. These phrases build confidence, recognize purpose, remind individuals of the ripple effects of their actions, and can instantly warm a student's heart and motivate that student (Harrison, 2022).

Celebrating our students outside the classroom becomes just as important as recognizing students' successes in the classroom. Taking and making time to attend a student's sporting event or theater performance outside of traditional classroom contexts can make a powerful statement to students. Additionally, when a student invites a teacher to their baseball game or choir performance, the teacher honors the student by accepting the invitation; in turn, the teacher may view the student through a fresh lens. Seeing a student who is quiet and unassuming in class, yet shines on the stage or playing field, gives a teacher a new and enlarged perspective of the student. What's more, watching a student hit a home run at a baseball game gives a teacher a point of connection with the student for the following day. Taking the time to invest in an after-school fundraiser or attend a band performance will give a teacher added clout with students. Showing up and supporting students' makes students feel seen and strengthens trust between teachers and students.

Intrigued by these connections, I often wonder about the places and spaces where I've been celebrated in juxtaposition with the places and spaces where I have overlooked an opportunity to celebrate others or have been overlooked myself. When I have missed an opportunity to celebrate a student, a friend, or a colleague, I have felt the impact. As teachers, we are keenly aware that we are in charge of our mindset and how we treat our students. We walk a fine line as we differentiate instruction and assess our students' needs and motivations in ways that honor both their academic and behavioral efforts. Observing and understanding students' strengths and areas for growth can help teachers build stronger and deeper connections with students. Classroom teacher Kimberly Parker recommends keeping a balanced approach to learning expectations for students; she suggests recognizing the ebb and flow of the school year while moving students forward with curriculum, while at the same time, offering students grace (2022). She recommends making peace with what doesn't seem to work for students so to encourage educators to elevate learning and highlight the special moments. Really looking at our classroom practices—whether related to daily routines or assessment practices—can help us demonstrate validation and care for students *and* may even help us celebrate students in new and creative ways.

Cultivating Celebration and Joy

Teachers regularly seek out and embrace new methods of teaching and sharing content. Teachers love students and love learning. There are so many aspects of teaching that bring me joy— and I am sure they bring you joy as well. I recently connected with a former student teacher named Elizabeth (a pseudonym). As we discussed her teaching, Elizabeth proclaimed, "teachers are nerds at heart" and yes, I think we are! Elizabeth enthusiastically admitted how much she "nerds out" when a science demonstration produces student wonder or when a student sees the relevance in a course reading. Joy-filled enthusiasm and shared celebration—whether it occurs during a math game or a historical role play—are contagious and have a ripple effect on our students.

Teachers don't and won't naturally possess each and every one of the 13 dispositions explored in *Dispositions Are a Teacher's Greatest Strength;* however, if you are an individual who intentionally strives to encourage others, you probably know how to celebrate (refer to Chapter 8 for more on the disposition of encouragement). Capitalizing on laughter, smiles, and humor is yet another opening that can lead to joy. Not every minute in the classroom is full of laughter, celebration or fun, but when a teacher adds a splash of fun or creativity, joy ensues. Brain breaks, games, or a creative instructional delivery with theatrics all work as strategies to stimulate joy in the classroom (Campbell, 2015). And when educators celebrate joy in their work, they remind themselves of their purpose, recognize their talents, celebrate their successes, and understand where they have come from. One of my student teachers, Carlos (a pseudonym), once shared with me that happiness is fleeting but joy sticks with you. He views joy as a long-lasting posture of the heart that lingers and permeates all facets of his being. When educators, like Elizabeth and Carlos, feel and share inner joy, they model for students and colleagues what it looks like to feel content and at home in their work and professional positions (Schwanke & Deagle, 2022).

As with the previous dispositions examined throughout this book, teachers can intentionally and enthusiastically choose to pursue celebration and joy. When teachers nurture these two dispositions, they cultivate interesting and thrilling learning experiences that can authentically increase their own vocational joy. Celebration and joy coexist as two unique treasures—each disposition must be developed and protected. I encourage you to share your passions, wisdom, and teaching experiences with your students and colleagues to bring on the celebration and joy! Are you ready to catch and ride the wave of celebration and joy?

Pause and Reflect

1. Consider the role of celebration in the classroom, when and how do you choose to celebrate student growth and progress?
2. Name three specific ways you can cultivate joy as a form of self-care and inspiration.
3. How do you feel when you are celebrated or recognized for your work or efforts? How might you transfer these contagious feelings to your students?
4. Name a circumstance when you overlooked a celebration for a class or a student. Do you regret the decision? Explain.
5. As you finish reading this chapter, reflect and identify two or three dispositions that bring you inner joy.

References

Campbell, K. (2015). Bringing the fun back to learning. *Association for Middle Level Education*. https://www.amle.org/bringing-the-fun-back-to-learning/

Costa, A. L., & Kallick, B. (2014). *Dispositions: Reframing teaching and learning*. Corwin.

Durwin, C. C., & Reese-Weber, M. J. (2017). *Ed psych modules* (3rd ed.). Sage.

Egbert, J. (2020). You are doing better than you think you are. *Association for Middle Level Education Magazine, 8*(4), 23–25. https://www.amle.org/youre-doing-better-than-you-think-you-are/

Frey, N. Hattie, J. & Fisher D. (2018). *Developing assessment capable visible learners grades K-12: maximizing skill, will and thrill*. Corwin.

Gallagher, J. (2023). Let's bring joy back into learning. *ASCD Blog*. https://www.ascd.org/blogs/lets-bring-joy-back-into-learning

Harrison, S. (2022). Use these 9 little phrases to instantly brighten someone's day, says happiness expert. *CNBC Make it*. https://www.cnbc.com/2022/11/22/say-these-little-phrases-to-instantly-brighten-someones-day-according-to-happiness-expert.html

Heider, K. L. (2005). Teacher isolation: How mentoring programs can help. *Current Issues in Education, 8*(14). https://cie.asu.edu/ojs/index.php/cieatasu/article/view/1686/725

Jensen, E. (2008). *Brain-based learning: The new paradigm of teaching* (2nd ed.). Corwin Press.

Mali, T. (2012). *What teachers make: In praise of the greatest job in the world*. The Penguin Group.

Merriam-Webster (2023). Celebration. Merriam-Webster.com Dictionary. https://www.merriam-webster.com/dictionary/celebration

Parker, K. N. (2022). Ending the school year strong. *ASCD Blog*. https://www.ascd.org/blogs/ending-the-school-year-strong

Radmacher, M. A. E. (2022). Celebrate kind ideas. Instagram. https://www.instagram.com/maryanneradmacher/

Rath, T., & Clifton, D. O. (2004). *How full is your bucket?* Gallup Press.

Santoro, D. A. (2019). The problem with stories about teacher burnout. *Kappan, 101*(4), 26–33. https://doi.org/10.1177/0031721719892971

Schwanke, J., & Deagle, T. R. (2022). Can we still find joy in teaching? *Educational Leadership.* https://www.ascd.org/el/articles/can-we-still-find-joy-in-teaching

Suh, C. (Director). (2023). *Working.* Netflix.

TED. (2013). Rita Pierson: *Every kid needs a champion* [Video]. YouTube. https://www.youtube.com/watch?v=SFnMTHhKdkw

Thornhill, S. S., & Badley, K. (2020). *Generating tact and flow for effective teaching and learning.* Routledge.

Torres, C. (2019). Assessment as an act of love. *ASCD Education Update* *61*(2). https://www.ascd.org/el/articles/assessment-as-an-act-of-love

Van Brummelen, H. (2012). Student assessment: Hitting the mark or lighting the candle? In K. Badley, & H. Van Brummelen (Eds.), *Metaphors we teach by: How metaphors shape what we do in the classroom* (pp. 89–108). Wipf and Stock.

14

Conclusion

Final Thoughts

After years of studying, thinking about, writing about, and talking about dispositions, I finally put pen to paper in the form of a book. What a joy! I love thinking about the dispositions that fill my professional cup and at the same time, I genuinely appreciate the opportunity to share these dispositions with my students, colleagues, and now you, my readers. My fundamental hope for *Dispositions Are a Teacher's Greatest Strength* is for teacher-readers to cultivate fresh perspective and energy. I hope that as you arrive at this final chapter, you have felt my offering of encouragement to grow professionally. *Dispositions Are a Teacher's Greatest Strength* shares hope-filled contexts, stories, and practical strategies to foster dispositional growth in educators, for those new to the profession or those with 30-plus years of experience. The book shines a light on 13 carefully curated dispositions; dispositions that I recommend for more than just career maintenance and survival. The 13 dispositions are needed for sustainability and career flourishing.

Dispositions Are a Teacher's Greatest Strength was written for educators in elementary and secondary schools, school and district administrators, pre-service program faculty, and those in higher education. This book is an invitation to engage with dispositions relevant to a teacher's daily work and practice. Whether readers are diving into their first teaching position or

DOI: 10.4324/9781003379539-14

are seasoned veterans, this book is written with the objective to energize and fuel you. Whether you read *Dispositions Are a Teacher's Greatest Strength* during the academic year, during the summer, in book groups, or even collectively as a school staff for teambuilding or at a professional development conference, the book is meant to uplift, inspire, and recharge your professional batteries. Each chapter authentically defines, identifies, and explores personal antidotes, research, and experiences related to a unique disposition. I am truly grateful that you chose to read about the dispositions I hold dear as well as the experiences and stories that I've accrued throughout my career.

Connecting the Dots and Dispositions

When I began writing this book, I thoughtfully considered the order of dispositions and chapters with the aim of presenting each disposition as a practical offering of refreshment to educators everywhere. About halfway through the writing progress, it became evident that the 13 dispositions I chose often lean on each other. Dispositions can stand alone but they appear stronger when they layer and weave together. Much like a tapestry that becomes stronger and more beautiful as its threads are sown together, a single disposition is a powerful and motivating tool for teaching, but a collection of dispositions truly becomes a teacher's greatest professional strength. For instance, when teachers engage in reflection, they often develop curiosity about other dispositions such as adaptability or collaboration, or they may recognize their own professional courage as they engage in reflection. Remarkably, developing the disposition of resilience in practice may lead a teacher to the disposition of hope; or nurturing gratitude may fuel a teacher's inner courage. Dispositions, whether examined individually or collectively, can help educators see the beauty, the progress, and the purpose behind the work they do.

I truly love the pedagogical facets of the work, planning curriculum, developing assessments, setting up classroom rotations, and creating engaging activities; yet, the heart part of teaching has always been the best and most significant aspect of the job for me. Studying dispositions later in my career when I arrived in higher education—reading, writing, discussing, and reflecting on dispositions—energizes me. Investing in and nurturing teaching dispositions or the softer heart skills strengthens all aspects of my teaching and professionalism; striving to model behaviors that we expect of students essentially nurtures these skills in me (Johnson, 2015). Timothy Kanold characterizes this aspect of our work as soul work because self-awareness adds depth to our professional lives (2021). According to Kanold, finding depth or meaning in our work and professional interactions sharpens our professional connections, responses, and perspectives.

Each fall, I bring in a stack of neatly wrapped (and empty) pizza boxes to share with my undergraduates. I borrowed the idea from a dear mentor and for over a decade, I have shared the activity with my students. Each pizza box is wrapped and labeled with an aspect of a teacher's job: curriculum, classroom management, professional development, grading and assessment, relationships, committee work. Before sharing this activity, I secretly ask a student volunteer to help me hold the first pizza box and then I add another box to the pile. And then I add another. As boxes are added, the student volunteer dramatically bends her knees to demonstrate that the pizza boxes are heavy; each additional pizza box intensifies the weight of the pile. The activity resonates with my students every time. Likewise, I hope that after reading *Dispositions Are a Teacher's Greatest Strength*, your "pizza boxes" and professional burdens feel lighter. Focusing on dispositions truly nourishes me and helps me see beyond the expected "pizza box tasks" of my daily work. Dispositions truly motivate me to recognize and reflect on the heart skills that we possess, develop, and share as teachers.

Chapter 2 in *Dispositions Are a Teacher's Greatest Strength* highlights the disposition of curiosity that sparks a teachers' love of learning, strengthens their own curiosity, and affirms the why behind choosing to teach. Chapter 2 encourages readers to consider how and when we recognize and see curiosity in ourselves and with our students. Chapter 3 follows and shines a light on developing a teacher's spirit of reflection; as you reach the end of this book, I am sure you recognize that reflection is an essential disposition for all teachers to nurture starting in their first days of teacher training. Whether a teacher journals each day, has a conversation with a colleague, or records reminders to strengthen a lesson on a post-it note, reflection weaves through every aspect of a teacher's work. Reflection's thread permeates every facet of a teacher's day even as it manifests in different ways and at different times.

The disposition of empathy stands tall as the star of Chapter 4. I am not sure how teachers can do their jobs without the disposition of empathy. Empathy gives educators the ability to connect to others' emotions and understand others' perspectives. Integral to a teacher's practice, empathy most often translates into experiencing another's feelings of distress while helping teachers respond with care and understanding. Adaptability follows (Chapter 5) as teachers acclimate, accommodate, adjust, and make hundreds of decisions each day in relationship to classroom culture, classroom management, content delivery, and assessment. Possessing the ability to pivot and remain flexible are skills that teachers demonstrate consistently in practice—often through challenging circumstances and student interactions.

Resilience, another disposition that consistently infiltrates teacher practice, is explored in Chapter 6. Teachers have always modeled resilience, but post-pandemic, resilience rises to the top of the dispositions' list. Gratitude, focused on in Chapter 7, follows resilience and encourages postures and mindsets that demonstrate appreciation. Reconnecting with an attitude of gratitude can give teachers and students an energizing boost.

Encouragement follows (Chapter 8) with a focus on cheering for both teachers and students. The disposition of encouragement can reciprocally strengthen a student's and teacher's confidence and motivation. Next, Chapter 9 meets the present moment with a focus on inclusion and creating welcome, highlighting and honoring all students fosters increased self-awareness and openness to others. Today's teachers and schools must take a no-excuses approach with the aim of cultivating inclusive classroom practices, school environments, and learning communities.

Unlike decades ago, teachers no longer function in figurative silos; instead, they are asked to develop relational skills for connection so they can learn from and share a collaborative spirit with others (Chapter 10). Today's teachers must be active and attentive listeners who consider how they handle conflict, use their professional voices, and respond to others. Chapter 11 next addresses the disposition of courage that teachers tap into daily with amazing dedication and strength. Courage stands as a non-negotiable disposition that occupies every aspect of a teacher's being. It takes enormous professional courage to show up every day, deal with the demands and challenges of the job, and care for students. The courageous work requires a generous amount of daily courage.

At the end of *Dispositions Are a Teacher's Greatest Strength*, three additional dispositions are explored (Chapters 12 and 13): hope, celebration, and joy. Belief in hope, as well as finding hope in our students and the future, drives us professionally. Looking for and identifying hope-filled moments in our work as well as the hopeful interactions with students inspires and validates a teacher's calling and decision to teach. Remarkably, pursuing the disposition of celebration can positively shift our attitude and cultivate joy. When we embrace opportunities to celebrate students, colleagues, and the wins in our classrooms and the profession, our cups overflow with a bit more joy. This chapter (Chapter 14) serves as the final bookend to the collection of dispositions first introduced in Chapter 1.

Dispositions Fuel the Heart

I sincerely hope that reading *Dispositions Are a Teacher's Greatest Strength* has offered you contexts and strategies to validate your work and replenish your soul. Whether you read the book in one sitting, chapter by chapter over a length of time, or if you skipped around between chapters, I offer encouragement and affirmation for the dispositional skills that you possess. If you are a new or an experienced teacher, I hope you feel hope-filled and rejuvenated. My desire as a writer is for you to consider and savor each disposition shared in this book. I trust you are able to reflect on your own professional journey to expand your self-awareness with confidence and fresh perspective so you can press on with authentic courage. Teaching requires a steadfast commitment and remains a life-long endeavor (Sherman, 2013, p. 145).

Years ago, editors William Schubert and William Ayers published a collection of narratives about teacher lore; they labeled teacher lore as the stories, reflections, and similarities in teaching as a framework that builds professional self-understanding in the classroom (1992). Teacher lore, whether individual or collaborative, can be a way of making sense of what we do as teachers and why we do it (Miller, 1992). I remain hopeful that this *Dispositions Are a Teacher's Greatest Strength* can serve and help educators teaching kindergarten or those in higher education, make sense of the work, its burdens, and joys. Dispositions grant meaning to our work and are the subtle ingredients that can fuel us, remind us of our purpose, and enlighten us. Dispositions are powerful strengths; "the more you use them, the more powerful they become—just like a muscle in your body" (Liesveld & Miller, 2005, p. 57). May each disposition in *Dispositions Are a Teacher's Greatest Strength* serve as encouragement to you so you are able to thrive and flourish professionally.

Berit Gordon, author of *The Joyful Teacher* (2020), observes teachers putting students' needs first, so much so, that they often don't have the energy to deal with the responsibilities and pressures they encounter in the profession. "We love our students and we care deeply about our jobs. And we are stressed, exhausted, and overwhelmed" (p. 1). Gordon stresses that teachers need to identify positive work experiences, engage in self-care, seek mentors, and stay away from unhealthy conversations because when teachers do so, they nurture and care for their inner selves. Setting goals, getting involved in what's going on outside of the classroom, advocating for students, studying personal biases, doing teacher research, reading books with colleagues, finding a mentor and asking, what will most help students? are additional suggestions for nurturing the self (pp. 285–291). Similarly, educator Todd Whitaker declares, "What makes teaching hard is that it matters every day" (2012, p. 47). Much like the common phrase, "Keep the main thing, the main thing," educators must remember what matters, remain focused, and stay the course. And dispositions are a necessary tool to help us remember what matters most.

Dispositions for Flourishing

Robert Fulghum, author of *All I Really Need to Know I Learned in Kindergarten*, has reminded readers for decades to play fair, be kind, and think of others (1986). As educators, we desire to pass on these reminders, similar behaviors, and habits to our students. Our classrooms provide rich contexts where students learn to not only read and write, but also keep their hands to themselves, share with others, think for themselves, and consider the needs of others. The work is challenging and feels monumental; whether we are teaching a history lesson or correcting a behavior, our students are developing social, academic, and emotional skills that they will carry with them into future classrooms, relationships, and careers. Enacting our calling to teach and develop dispositional habits and skills in our students is no small endeavor.

As teachers and students engage in dispositional development, the more dispositions become internalized in their minds, hearts, and behaviors (Costa et al., 2021, p. 62). Hence, the heart and soul of every educator need to be attended to; people need to feel like they are important and make a difference (Laskowski, 2023). When educators activate the dispositions explored in this book, their frustrations and fears often fall away. Placing a focus on dispositions remains a proactive approach for sustaining positivity and momentum in the profession in today's educational climate. Dispositions truly ground us and at the same time they give us a place to return to when we need a reset, are feeling drained, or misunderstood. "Professional teacher dispositions give teachers, teacher educators, administrators, and educational researchers a language that can be used to talk about and describe what teachers do and what makes them do what they do" (Kruger-Ross, 2014, p. 161).

Each spring, as my student teachers finish up pre-service program requirements, I ask them to consider the impact of the program's four core dispositions on their professional practice. Responses often include, "Dispositions bring the humanity into teaching" or "Dispositions can prevent burnout and center teachers who, by no fault of their own, can get caught up in the routine tasks, daily demands and expected to do lists." One particular student teacher, Matthew (a pseudonym), wowed me when he framed dispositions as "actions in development" explaining that "dispositions are why you teach. Dispositions are authentic and genuine self-checks; they are a means to care for the teacher-self."

Dispositions elevate our understanding of the heart part of our work that weaves through each facet of the job. We bring our whole selves to our classrooms with our hearts on full display. We demonstrate *curiosity* when we invite student inquiry and we engage in thoughtful *reflection* as we contemplate how to hook students into learning. We offer *empathy* when we listen to a woeful student and we demonstrate *adaptability* when we gracefully adjust to a new schedule. One minute, we display *resilience* after a lockdown drill and the next moment we express *gratitude* for a colleague. We regularly deliver *encouragement* to students with a broad smile, a handshake, or a high-five. We also greet students with an *inclusive* invitation to provide them with a sense belonging. In addition, as we engage *collaboratively* on school committees, we share *courage* and *hope* with a steady presence and optimistic outlook. Finally, we infuse *celebration* and *joy* throughout our lessons with a spirit of openness and opportunity. These 13 dispositions—the attitudes, postures, and commitments of the heart—demonstrate the immeasurable amount of teacher-care we can offer to students, our school communities, and ourselves. Borrowing the words of Ken Badley, "Teachers come to school with both their classes and their souls prepared" (2012, p. 156). When pursued and practiced, dispositions truly emerge as a teacher's greatest professional strength.

As a final nod to Parker Palmer, I uphold dispositions as conduits for the soul work that stimulates and replenishes a teacher's heart (2017). Engaging in dispositional work stands as an honorable and worthy endeavor for developing new teachers and sustaining experienced teachers. Whether you are new to the profession or are counting your years of service, I hope you thoroughly enjoyed your journey through *Dispositions Are a Teacher's Greatest Strength*. I trust you feel a spark (or two) of inspiration from joining the head and heart of teaching for professional flourishing. With unique professional challenges before us, we can choose to clench our fists and stomp our feet as we care for students or we can choose to open our hearts to learn, develop, and share dispositions generously—*dispositions ARE our greatest strength*. Thank you for accepting the invitation to read, reflect, and journey with me.

Pause and Reflect

1. Which of the 13 dispositions highlighted in *Dispositions Are a Teacher's Strength* do you plan to pursue and develop in practice?
2. Identify two dispositions that ground you professionally.
3. How and when might you share and pass on what you have learned about dispositions with colleagues?
4. Consider how specific dispositions in this book can invigorate your professional practice.
5. Are you ready to commit to implementing dispositional development as a form of self-care?

References

Badley, K. (2012). Metaphors and models of faith learning integration. In K. Badley, & H. Van Brummelen (Eds.), *Metaphors we teach by: How metaphors shape what we do in classrooms* (pp. 139–156). Wipf and Stock.

Costa, A. L., Kallick, B., & Zmuda, A. G. (2021). Building a culture of efficacy with habits of mind. *Educational Leadership, 79*(3), 57–62. https://www.ascd.org/el/articles/building-a-culture-of-efficacy-with-habits-of-mind

Fulghum, R. (1986). *All I really need to know I learned in kindergarten: Uncommon thoughts on common things*. Ivy Books.

Gordon, B. (2020). *The joyful teacher*. Heinmen Publishers.

Johnson, L. (2015). *Teaching outside the box: How to grab your students by their brains* (3rd ed.). Jossey-Bass.

Kanold, T. D. (2021). *Soul! Fulfilling the promise of your professional life as a teacher and leader*. SolutionTree.

Kruger-Ross, M. J. (2014). Ways of being as an alternative to the limits of teacher dispositions. In J. A. Gorlewski, D. A. Gorleswski, J. Hopkins, & B. J. Porfilio (Eds.), *Effective or wise?* (pp. 155–173). Peter Lang.

Laskowski, T. (2023). In organizational change efforts, belonging matters. *Educational Leadership, 80*(6), 10. https://www.ascd.org/el/articles/in-organizational-change-efforts-belonging-matters

Liesveld, R., & Miller, J. A. (2005). *Teach with your strengths: How great teachers inspire their students*. Gallup Press.

Miller, J. L. (1992). Teachers' spaces. In W. H. Schubert, & W. C. Ayers (Eds.), *Teacher lore: Learning from our own experience* (pp. 11–22). Longman.

Palmer, P. (2017). *The courage to teach*. Jossey-Bass.

Schubert, W. H., & Ayers, W. C. (1992). *Teacher lore: Learning from our own experience*. Longman.

Sherman, S. C. (2013). *Teacher preparation as an inspirational practice: Building capacities for responsiveness*. Routledge.

Whitaker, T. (2012). *What great teachers do differently: 17 things that matter most* (2nd ed.). Eye on Education.

Index